POONA

IN BYGONE DAYS

POONA IN BYGONE DAYS

RAO BAHADUR D. B. PARASNIS

GYAN

Published by

Gyan Publishing House
5, Ansari Road
Daryaganj, New Delhi-110002
Phone: 011-47034999, 9811692060
E-mail: books@gyanbooks.com

Distribution Network
gyanbooks.com
India, USA, Canada, UK, Australia, France

ISBN : 978-81-212-9460-7 (PB)
First Published, 1921

2nd Impression 2023

Printed at: Gyan Press, Delhi.

POONA IN BYGONE DAYS
Author: RAO BAHADUR D. B. PARASNIS

SHIVAJI, THE FOUNDER OF THE MARATHA EMPIRE.

POONA IN BYGONE DAYS

BY

RAO BAHADUR D. B. PARASNIS

Author of "Mahableshwar," etc.

BOMBAY

THE TIMES PRESS

1921

THIS BOOK

IS

RESPECTFULLY DEDICATED

TO

HIS EXCELLENCY THE RIGHT HON'BLE

SIR GEORGE LLOYD,

G.C.I.E., D.S.O.,

GOVERNOR OF BOMBAY,

WITH HIS GRACIOUS PERMISSION.

CONTENTS

LIST OF ILLUSTRATIONS

PREFACE

THE keen interest now-a-days shown in historical research and old monuments by European and Indian scholars alike has encouraged me to collect information about Poona and its historical sites from all available sources. In addition to material taken from unpublished old records I have culled extracts from old and rare books which possess peculiar interest—some of the extracts being the writings of great men, such as Elphinstone, Malcolm, Price, Moor, etc., who took actual part in the political transactions at Poona or were eye-witnesses of the scenes enacted there at the end of the eighteenth century. This first instalment I now venture to put before the public on the memorable occasion of H.R.H. the Prince of Wales' visit to Poona, and I hope that my humble effort will be of some use to those who desire to know something of Poona and its early history.

I beg to offer my sincere and respectful thanks to H. E. Sir George Lloyd, Governor of Bombay; who has taken keen interest in the excavation and preservation of the famous Shanwar Wada and has extended to me his sympathy and help in bringing out the present publication. I am grateful to my esteemed friend, the Hon'ble Mr. C. A. Kincaid, C.V.O., I.C.S., for kindly consenting to write a short introduction to this book and for giving me several useful suggestions.

The illustrations in this book are chiefly taken from original pictures and photographs in my historical collection at Satara ; and I am greatly indebted to Mr. R. D. Banerji, M.A., Superintendent, Archæological Survey, Western Circle, Poona, for the valuable help he has rendered me in their reproduction.

Happy Vale,
Satara.

D. B. P.

GANPATI RANG-MAHAL—PESHWA'S DARBAR IN 1790.

Poona in Bygone Days.

I.

SHANWAR WADA.

THE Shanwar Wada was the most magnificent and stately mansion that was ever built in Poona by the Peshwas in the 18th century. The foundation stone of the building was laid by Bajirao I (1720-1740) on Saturday, the 10th of January 1730, being an auspicious day. On this occasion, according to state records, Rs. 1-8 were spent in charity. There is an interesting legend about the site selected for this historic building. While riding over this ground, the Peshwa Bajirao saw, to his great astonishment, a hare chasing a hound, which struck to his mind that there must be something very auspicious in this place, where a hare forgetting its natural timidity boldly chased a dog. He at once resolved to secure the site and build there a house for himself and his family. At that time, this piece of land was included in the '*Kasba*' or village of Poona which was enclosed by a mud wall. It contained only a few huts of fishermen and weavers, from whom Bajirao acquired five acres of land by exchanging them for suitable sites in Mangalwar Peith and commenced the building rapidly. Within an interval of two years a two storeyed Palace with three quadrangles sprung up to be the focus and centre of all the life and movement of the Maratha power. The opening ceremony of the Palace was performed according to Hindu religious customs on Saturday, the 22nd January 1732, when Rs. 15½ were paid in charity to Brahmans. It is stated that the total expenditure incurred on this Palace came up to Rs. 16,110.

As conceived originally the plan of the Palace was very simple and elegant and only the *Diwan Khana* or the main hall of audience contained some ornamental carvings. It was the third Peshwa, Balaji Bajirao (1740-1761), who made several additions and alterations, and added much splendour and beauty to this fine mansion. He devoted his store of knowledge as well as money and patience in turning out this edifice to be an object of great delight and admiration. Later on, Nana Phadnawis, Prime Minister to Sawai Madhavrao (1774-1795), constructed a few more rooms and halls, galleries and towers, pavilions and fountains, and made the royal residence truly majestic and grand, worthy of the great rulers of Maharashtra.

The Palace was destroyed by fire in 1827 and now there remain only the fortified enclosure wall, and the five gateways, and nine bastions. It is therefore impossible to form a correct idea of the actual building which existed in the hey-day of the Peshwa's power. The foundations of the Palace and various other buildings in the extensive compound which covers about five acres of ground have been recently unearthed by the Archæological Department. They give us a faint idea of the original plans of the building but no picture of the real magnificence and greatness of this royal mansion. It is said that only one mirror-hall survived the great fire of 1827, but that too was scattered owing to the want of historical interest in these days. It is only latterly that Government have been taking great interest in the preservation of objects of historical and archæological interest, and thanks to H. E. Sir George Lloyd, whose genuine interest and wonderful energy have enabled us to see the old foundations and remains of the Peshwa's Palace, which were buried under heaps of debris for nearly a century.

The main building of the Palace consisted of six storeys and it is said that the spire of the Alandi temple could be seen from the uppermost terrace of this building. Sawai Madhavrao

Peshwa used to enjoy a beautiful view of the Parvati temple and of the city from the terrace of his *Meghadambari* room, and often spend evening hours looking at the stars in the sky through a telescope which was presented to him by Sir Charles Malet, the British Resident at his Court. The height of the main building can be imagined by the height of the existing *Nagarkhana* (music gallery) from the top of which the royal standard of the Peshwas waved proudly day and night. The main entrance to the Palace is known as Delhi Gate as it faces Delhi in the north. Raja Shahu of Satara told Bajirao I not to put the main entrance to the north as it would mean a disrespect to the Mogul Emperor of Delhi, whom Raja Shahu held in great respect and to whom he acknowledged his allegiance. In deference to the wishes of his master the Peshwa stopped the work ; and the present massive gate which still indicates the former greatness of this Palace was the work of Bajirao's son, Balaji, who completed it in 1751 after Raja Shahu's death. It may be worthy of note here that the design of the entrance gate is exactly a copy of that of Indraprastha, the ancient Hindu capital of the Pandawas, in old Delhi. The Peshwas, being devoted Hindus, selected the design of the gate of Indraprastha, or Purana Killa, instead of imitating the magnificent gates of the Mogul capital.

As mentioned above the Palace had five principal gates and they were named as follows :—

1. Delhi Darwaja—as it faces the north.
2. Ganesh Darwaja—as it was near the famous Ganpati Mahal.
3. Mastani Darwaja—which is mentioned in old records as Natakshala gate was named after Mastani, the beautiful mistress of Bajirao I, who was brought from Raja Chhatrasal of Bundelkhand. Nana Phadnawis afterwards called it 'Ali Bahadur Darwaja' after the grandson of Mastani, who conquered Bundelkhand and founded the Banda State.
4. Khidki Darwaja—which was always closed and the entrance was open through a small window. This Darwaja is now known as 'Kavathi' on account of a *Kavathi* tree grown near it.
5. Jambul Darwaja—owing to a tree of *Jambul*.

Of the four fortified walls two measured 200 yards in length and 20 feet in height, two 150 yards of the same height. They contained in all nine bastions built of stone below and brick above, of which four are at the corners and five in the middle of the rampart. Their names with the number of their guards are given below :—

1.	Bastion Delhi Darwaja ..	20	soldiers.
2.	Bastion Ali Bahadur Darwaja	10	,,
3.	Bastion Corner I ..	20	,,
4.	Bastion Dindi Darwaja ..	10	,,
5.	Bastion Khidki Darwaja..	15	,,
6.	Bastion Corner II ..	10	,,
7.	Bastion Side Corner of Ganesh Darwaja ..	15	,,
8.	Bastion North Corner of Ganesh Darwaja ..	25	,,
9.	Bastion Jambul Darwaja.	20	,,

Besides the above there were patrols at ten more points making the total on the rampart 275 men.

The Palace contained four large courts or *chouks* and several halls or state-rooms known as "Diwan-khanas." They had taken their names from their decorations or other uses. The most important halls were as follows :—

1. Ganpati Rang-mahal—Hall of audience.
2. Nachāchā Diwankhana—Dancing hall.

3. Arsè Mahal—Hall of mirrors.
4. Junā Arsè Mahal—Old Hall of mirrors.
5. Dadasahebānchā Diwankhana—Hall of Raghunathrao Peshwa.
6. Thorlyā Rāyāchā Diwankhana—Hall of the first Peshwa.
7. Narayan Ravāchā Mahal—Hall of Narayanrao Peshwa.
8. Hastidanti Mahal—Ivory hall.

Besides these there were many other rooms and apartments assigned to different members of the royal family and to several departments of the household such as Treasury, Store room, Record room, Library, Jewellery room, Armoury room, Medicine room, etc., etc. The vast household was well regulated and controlled, separate officers being appointed for the supervision and management of the Palace. There were regular guards and patrols placed inside and outside of the Palace. As the records show, the staff at the Palace in 1779 contained the following :—

480 Royal Guards,
229 Purandar Guards,
325 Kanadi Infantry,
34 Attendants of Royal Stables,
82 Royal Cavalry-men,

224 Infantry men,
76 Attendants,
1,690 Shiledars and bargirs

Thus making up a total of 3,144. In addition to this there were 300 regular sowars or horse-soldiers in attendance night and day. This number afterwards rose to 500. Such was the strength of the Royal household of the Peshwas.

As regards the construction and style of the Diwankhanas or halls of this Palace, it may be said that they were generally of one pattern—"*Kalamdani*" meaning an oblong old inkstand fashion, one central hall with flat ceiling and small compartments with sloping ceiling on four sides. The ornamentation was generally of one pattern. The pillars supporting the main hall were beautifully carved out and shaped like cypress trees, and joined together on the top by engraved arches of exquisite workmanship. The ceilings were covered with beautiful wooden tracery in different designs and were painted with trees, creepers, flowers, or scenes from the great epics, the Mahabharat and the Ramayan. Bhojraj, a very skilful artist from Jaypur, was specially engaged for the work of painting these halls.

The main Diwankhana or the Durbar hall in this Palace was the Ganpati Ranga-mahal. It was

GANPATI PROCESSION

(A PAINTING BY THE PUPILS FROM THE PESHWA'S CHITRASHALA OR SCHOOL OF ART.)

designed and built by Balaji Bajirao, the third Peshwa, for celebrating Ganpatı Festival, in 1755. This historic hall was the scene of many political and social events and the famous picture of the Poona Durbar represents the remarkable assembly held here in 1791. Captain Moor who visited Poona when the Peshwa's power was at its height describes the splendour of this hall in the following words :—

> " He (the Peshwa) has a very magnificent room in his palace at Poona, called the Ganes room, in which, on particular festivals in honour of Ganes, he receives numerous visitors ; I have seen more than a hundred dancing girls in it at one time. At one end, in a recess, is a fine gilt figure, I believe in marble, of this deity, and many other mythological decorations around it ; the other end of the room, bounded by a narrow strip of water in which fountains play, is open to a garden of fragrant flowers, which, combined with the murmuring of the fountains, has a very pleasing effect. This room is well designed in Mr. Daniel's fine picture of the Poona Durbar unrivalled perhaps in oriental grouping, character, and costume. This picture was painted for Sir Charles Malet, from sketches by the late Mr. Wales ; and the artist has chosen the time

when Sir Charles, then our Ambassador at the Court of Poona, attended by his suite, delivered to His Highness the Peshwa, in full Durbar, the treaty of alliance, ratified by his Majesty, between Great Britain and His Highness ; made, preparatory to the war between the triple allied powers and Tippoo, in 1790."

Robert Mabon, a European artist, who helped Mr. Wales in preparing the sketches of the Poona Durbar and visited the Ganpati Mahal in his company about this period (1790-1795) has given a most graphic description of the Poona Durbar.

"During my stay at Poona," writes Mr. Mabon, "I had the pleasure of being introduced to the durbar, or court of the Mahrattas. After waiting there some time, in conference with several Brahmins, attendants of the Peshwa, he made his appearance. I made a salam to him, which he gracefully returned, and advanced to the musnud or throne ; on which he sat down, cross-legged, with attendants behind him, armed with swords ; one of whom was his chowree-bardar, with a large chowree, or whisk, in his hand to keep off the flies. In front of the Peshwa stood his chopdar, with a long silver stick, ready to receive any orders he might be pleased to favour him with.

"I sat down at a distance in the attitude in which the Peshawa was, *viz*: cross-legged, as nothing is considered by him a greater piece of impoliteness than extending your legs, or sitting in any manner in which the soles of your feet might be pointed towards him. He was of a fair complexion and appeared to be about twenty-three years of age; his dress consisted of a long jama, or gown, of very fine muslin; a string of very large pearls hung from his neck, a considerable way down his waist; a very fine red shawl, with a rich embroidered border, was thrown carelessly over his shoulders, wore a beautiful cluster of diamonds, the centre one of which was about an inch square, of a very fine water. On the top of his turban, he wore a small curvature of gold, about three inches high, richly set with emeralds and various precious stones; over the right temple, from the top of the turban, hung several strings of pearls, which terminated at bottom by small red tassels. In this group, on the left, I was introduced to Nana Furanvese, his then Prime Minister, and formerly regent during the time the Peshwa was under age. It is to this sagacious politician, that almost all ascribe the present flourishing state of the

Mahratta empire. His dress was much the same with that of the Peshwa, but not so splendid.

"The musnud, or throne, is raised from the ground about four inches, and consists simply of three pillows covered with dark green velvet, placed upon rich embroidered cloth, in the manner represented in the annexed sketch. Before the Peshwa, upon this cloth is placed his *cuttar* (Katyar) or dagger, beautifully enamelled with various devices: next to it, a small urn and plate, made of copper, enamelled, and his goolab-danee for sprinkling rose-water, richly set with diamonds; close to them, his betelnut-box, which is truly splendid, it is set so full of diamonds, that at a little distance, it appears entirely composed of them: next to it is placed a silver cup, for his saliva, on a towel; and last of all, his sword and shield; the handle of the sword is green enamelled, full of diamonds; the scabbard is covered with red scarlet; the shield differs in no respect from the common Mahratta one, otherwise than that the five studs upon it, are gold; which, in that of a person of inferior rank, would be plated, or perhaps plain brass.

" . . . . The room in which the Peshwa thus sits in state, has nothing of beauty or elegance to recommend it : on one side, is a row of wooden pillars, over which are hung purdahs, made of kincobs, or gilt flowered silk, which are so constructed as to bind up or let down as occasion may require. Opposite to these pillars, are a few windows made in the eastern mode, very narrow and long. The Durbar is a very extensive building built in a style peculiar to the Asiaticks in general.

" In surveying the Peshwa seated on the musnud, the eye is dazzled with the immense riches about him ; but his effeminate dress and unmanlylike attitude which the customs of the people make him under the necessi y of observing, takes away from that dignity in appearance, which an European might expect to see in a Prince seated on a throne. After remaining sometime with the Peshwa, betelnut was presented me, which according to their custom, is the signal to depart. I accordingly, after accepting of it, took my leave."

The Ganpati Ranga-mahal may be styled as the 'Diwan-i-am' of the Marathas, as it had seen many vicissitudes of fortune and witnessed many important events of great consequence. Here the great festival in honour of Ganpati was celebrated with *eclat* every year in the bright half of Bhadrapad which lasted for ten days. Here the Dasara Durbar was held annually on a very grand scale when all the sardars and military officers assembled to pay their homage to the Peshwa. The great Peshwa, Balaji Bajirao, celebrated his glorious victories in the north and south of India in this very building. His son Madhavrao I tried to regain the lost glories of the Marathas in the battle of Panipat by his judicious and wise rule in this Palace. His brother and successor Narayanrao was cruelly murdered in a corner room of the main building. His posthumous son, Sawai Madhavrao, resided here nearly for twenty memorable years, while the administration was carried on under the sole guidance of the famous minister Nana Phadnawis. His brilliant courts in the Ganpati Rang-mahal were thronged not only by sardars and chiefs from different parts of the Maratha Empire, but by representatives and envoys of European Nations and other Indian States. The marriage of the Peshwa was celebrated here with great pomp in 1782 and the Nizam of Hyderabad, the Raja of Nagpur, the Raja of Satara and other Chiefs and Sardars from all parts of India attended the grand ceremony. The state entry of Sawai Madhavrao in Poona after the victory over the Nizam at Kharda in 1795 was the last exhibition of Maratha glory and power, which passed away with the death of the young Peshwa by an accidental fall from the first story of the Ganpati Mahal on a fountain in the same year. It may be interesting to note that all the ambassadors and representatives of the foreign powers were received and political business was transacted with them in this very Durbar hall. It is stated in old records that two members of the Bombay Council, Thomas Byfeld and John Spencer, were received here by Balaji Bajirao in 1756 and given dresses of honour worth Rs. 1,224. Here Mr. Mostyn, Col. Upton, and many other English gentlemen were received with honour and were presented with rich dresses and ornaments. It is said that Mr. Mostyn was charmed with the fragrance of the Peshwa's rose-water and expressed a desire to have a bottle or two for his use, but to his surprise next day, orders were issued to supply him half a pound of best rose water every day as long as he remained in Poona. The French representatives, M. Bussy and St. Lubin, were given audience in the same hall and received costly presents from the Peshwa. Since the establishment of the British Residency in Poona in 1786

Sir Charles Malet and his suite were the constant visitors to the Durbar. They cultivated great friendship with the Marathas and kept up cordial relations with them.

This hall as well as others were surrounded by beautiful rows of fountains that used to play here on festive occasions. It may be noted that in India it was the custom from ancient times to erect fountains and gardens in Royal Palaces for the sake of pleasure, art, and beauty, and the Mogul Palaces at Lahore, Delhi, and Agra are specially famous for their magnificent gardens and ornamental fountains. The Moguls and Hindus like other Eastern nations were interested in art, and enjoyed beauty not for selfish purpose, but for religious and traditional ideas which they cherished most. The Peshwas too following the example of the Mogul princes adorned their palaces with beautiful gardens and water fountains, terraces, and pavilions. There are yet some traces of original fountains which confirm our belief that they were imitated from Mogul palaces in Northern India. Besides a number of fountains and gardens for ornamental purposes, the Poona Palace had some special fountains constructed most artistically and ingeniously for the pleasure and joy of the Peshwa, Sawai Madhavrao. There was one celebrated fountain known as "Hazari Karanjè" or thousand sprayed fountain in the western side of the main Palace which was an object of curiosity and wonder to the whole court. It had the shape of a lotus flower of sixteen petals—each petal having sixteen spouts with a circumference of 80 feet. It is said that in India there is not a single fountain like this anywhere having 196 jets, not even in Europe, excepting the celebrated fountain 'Fontana di Trevi' at Rome. The water of this great fountain played in hundred patterns while the sun for its amusement would make and break a thousand rainbows. Like the Diana's Fountain at Versailles it was a favourite rendezvous of the Poona Durbar and the young Peshwa Sawai Madhavrao was an enthusiastic lover of this wonderful sight. In the western side near the Ganapati Hall, there was another deep tank or well, built after the Mogul pattern, to exhibit shining waterfalls. The stone-chutes were so ingeneously cut that the water running over them was thrown down forcibly and broken into ripples and splashes. They were called "Chadars" meaning white shawls of water. Behind these transparent waterfalls a skilful arrangement was made to place coloured lights in the niches which gave a charmingly brilliant effect at night. The young Peshwa was very fond of these shows and used to invite his Royal guests to enjoy the delightful scene. It is on record that he had invited one of the Patwardan Sardars to see this marvellous water "Chadar" in 1780.

In this Palace the state rooms or Durbar halls were lofty and well arranged, and contained very rich articles of furniture and tapestry. The department of jewellery and library contained choicest and rarest things. The picture gallery possessed most valuable masterpieces of the old Mogul and Persian arts, and also finest specimens of old masters in Europe, mostly presents from foreign Nations such as the English, the French, and the Portuguese. The armoury was full of rare and curious arms, and the collection of arts and curios was placed in the Museum Hall known as *Jinnas Khana.* It contained chiefly foreign articles of art and mechanism including watches, clocks, globes, music boxes, and toys. According to oriental fashion these halls were tastefully arranged and decorated with wall paintings and were the objects of great admiration to those who had the good fortune to visit them.

This brief account will hardly give a real idea of the pomp and glory of this historic building which it once possessed in the zenith of the Peshwa's power. Among Marathi records there are no descriptions preserved of this Palace, but fortunately they have been recorded by a few European gentlemen who visited the Poona Durbar on diplomatic mission or with an object of curiosity. Their accounts place vividly before our eyes a graphic picture of the old scenes of the Palace, and it is hoped that the following extracts will be found highly interesting.

The first among the visitors was Major Price who visited Poona in 1791. He commanded a grenadier company in Captain Little's battalion and with it joined the Maratha army under the Brahmin General, Parashuram Bhow. He was present in the battle of Dharwar against Tipu Sultan in 1791, where he was severely wounded. On the surrender of Dharwar he proceeded to Poona where he remained attached to the military guard, or honorary escort, of Sir Charles Malet, first British Resident at the Peshwa's Court, until the Peace of Seringapatam. He visited the Peshwa's Palace on several occasions in company with Sir Charles Malet. He describes his visit on the 7th April 1791 in the following terms:—

"The Resident, attended by the whole of his suite, European and native,and preceded by the escort of sepoys—about 80 in number—crossed the ford of the Moota; and proceeding through the middle of the crowded city, we came to the entrance of the Palace, which looks to the east*. This leading through a lofty gateway we passed to the left, along a very ordinary colonnade, which appeared, indeed, as yet in an unfinished state ; and at the termination of this, a sharp turn to the right, brought us at once into the Dewankhanah or hall of audience. This was spacious and lofty, but perfectly simple, and without ornament, unless we except the usual carving in the woodwork. The side towards the area—which as far as I recollect was to the north—was entirely open, the roof being sustained by wooden pillars ; and the floor was covered, from end to end, with a spotless piece of white calico. The young Prince was seated on his regal cushion—or gaddy, his Minister, the veteran and intelligent Nana Furnoveis, on his right hand, and other functionaries, and military chiefs, forming a semi-circle at the head, and one side, of the saloon.

" As we were, in conformity with prior arrangements, all in satin shoes and silk stockings, we advanced without interruption, being, of course, announced by numerous choubdaurs, or silver sticks, towards the Prince, who stood up to receive us ; and having treated

---

*Ganesh Darwaja.

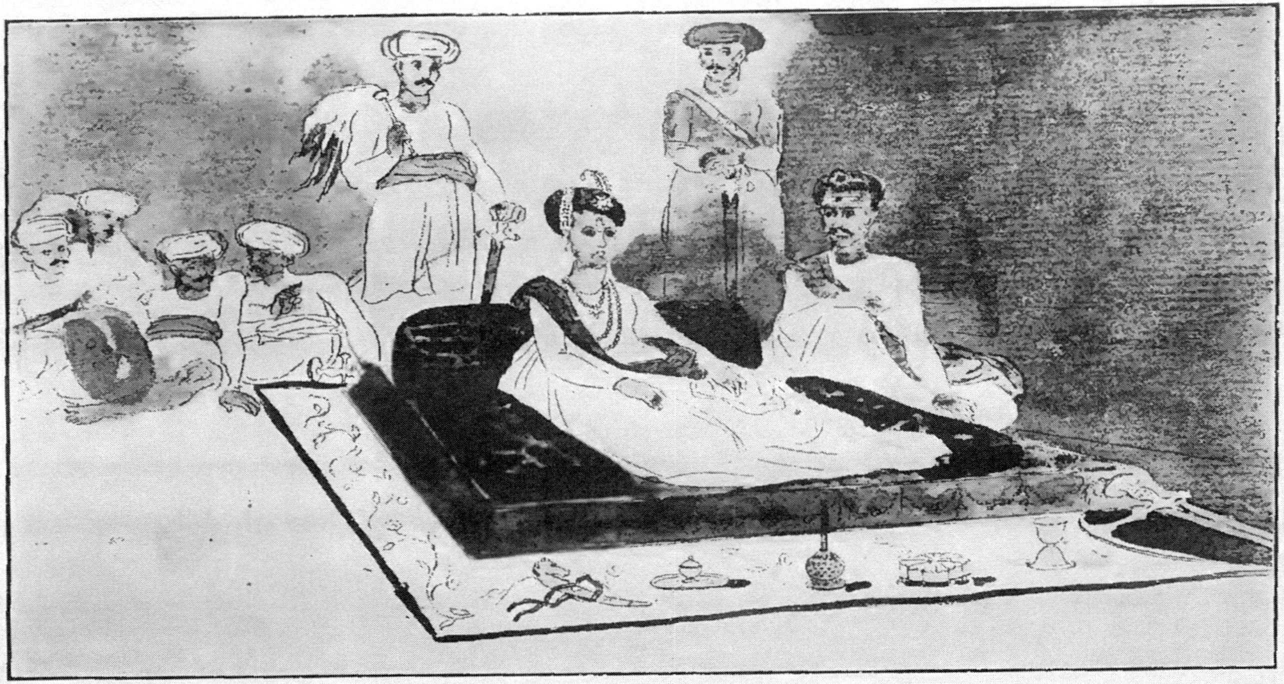

SAWAI MADHAVRAO PESHWA AND HIS MINISTER NANA PHADNAVIS.

each of us, without exception, with the buggulguiry, or accolade—which was also done by the Minister—we all of us then seated ourselves, as best we could, upon our hams—as much as possible concealing the soles of our shoes, which it would have been considered the extreme of indecorum to discover.

"The Resident, communicated with the Peshwa, through the Minister, in a manner which appeared most cordial and unreserved. And I cannot forget the splendid display of jewels which decorated the person of the young Prince ; but more particularly a superb necklace, descending far down the breast, and consisting of alternate diamonds and emeralds each fully as large as a nut-meg ; which must have been of inestimable value."

Another distinguished visitor Lord Valentia, who paid a visit to Poona in 1803, has left an interesting account of it in his travels. About the Palace he writes :—

"On entering the Palace, we found His Highness's cavalry and guard of infantry drawn out, with his elephants and suwarry ; they were by no means splendid. As we passed under the Nobit Khanah the kettle-drums beat. Within the walls the servants were all at their posts, and the crowd considerable. In the windows were numbers of the higher orders. We quitted our palanquins at the foot of the stairs, which we mounted, attended only by our Chobdars and Ausubadars. A small anti-room led to the durbar. At the door, I waited a few seconds, till I saw that the Dewan of the State, Sadaseeo Maunkesor, was sufficiently near; when, having quitted my slippers, I stepped on the white cloth with which the whole room was covered, Colonel Close supporting my left arm. I embraced the Dewan, and presented the officers of my suite. At this moment the Peshwa entered the room, and stepped on his guddi or throne.

"The Palace is a tolerable handsome building, and was very clean. The Durbar room is large; it is supported by wooden pillars handsomely carved. His guddi was of white muslin, richly embroidered in gold and coloured silk. His attendants stood round without the pillars, except a few with silver sticks. Holkar did not much injure the Palace, but he carried away every thing moveable; a small armoury and the elephant haudahs did not escape."

Sir James Mackintosh, Recorder of the Bombay Court, paid a visit to the Peshwa in 1805. He describes the Palace in his journal as follows :—

" We went about half a mile, or somewhat less, through the city, of which the principal streets are paved with flags, and which is reckoned one of the best-built native towns in India. The word *Bhara* (*wada* ?) which is the term for the Peshwa's house, ought not to be translated palace, because it is applied also to the houses of the other Mahratta Chiefs at Poona. From its size, it might well deserve the name ; the front is about the length of Somerset-house towards the Strand. We entered through a gate into a large square formed by the *Bhara*. The walls all around were painted with scenes of Hindu mythology. At one of the corners of this rather handsome square, we had a staircase to climb, which formed a singular contrast to the exterior of the building ; it was steeper than that which goes to the terrace at Parell, and not half so broad. At the top of this staircase was the entry of the hall of audience, where I left the splendidly embroidered slippers with which Colonel Close had furnished me. The hall was a long gallery, about the length perhaps of the verandah at Parell, but somewhat wider, supported by two rows of handsome wooden pillars, either of oak or of some timber exactly resembling it. (The width of which I speak is between the pillars.) Behind the pillars, on each side was a recess about half the breadth of the middle part. This apartment was carpeted, and near the end at which we entered was a white cloth laid, with three pillows: this was the Musnud, or throne."

From the above description it appears that Bajirao did not receive his illustrious guest in the Ganpati Mahal but in another hall, which is difficult to distinguish from others at this distance of time.

The fourth English gentleman to describe the Palace was Lt.-Col. Fitzclarence who visited Poona on the 31st January 1818, shortly after the battle of Kirkee, when the Peshwa Bajirao had already left Poona and the Palace was occupied by the British and turned into a military hospital. He writes :—

" The old Palace is surrounded with a wall and circular bastions, having an open space in its front. The walls of an inner court are miserably daubed with the Hindoo mythology, elephants, and horsemen. His Highness made but little use of this abode except on public occasions, though it contained the temple or room for the yearly fête in hōnour of his protecting deity Gunish.

" I found Mr. Coates in a deep verandah in one of the small courts, crowded with trees and shrubs, and he was so good as to shew us round the Palace. The great quadrangle is more handsome than that at Nagpoor, has sculptured wood pillars and cornices, which are very splendid, and the whole Palace is glazed throughout. A very fine room. with dark-coloured wooden pillars, and carpeted with red cloth stuffed with cotton, displayed a full length picture of the Marquis Wellesely, which had been found neglected in a small adjacent apartment ; and near the likeness of this great statesman was a miniature of Sir Barry Close, also found in the palace, let into the wall in the plaster. There were also two very large well-fashioned globes, with the names in the Latin language, and also the . . . of silver. These, it was supposed, had been a present from the King of England to a former Peshwa, previous to the year 1788. From the top of the Palace I had a most extensive view of the city, camp, mango groves, the ruins of the Sungum, and holy hill of Parbutty, to the south-east of the city. Poona, not having any suburb like Nagpoor, is inferior in population, and covers less ground.

"We now proceeded to the holy chamber, dedicated to a deity who could boast of an elephant's head and trunk, and who, to complete the interest he excited, was painted blue. He was sitting cross-legged, but we did not find this sapient gentleman ready to receive us, for after rummaging about, he was discovered put by in a cupboard, to keep him from the dirt and flies. The room is vaulted, and about fifty feet along, and very high, with a gallery which runs round it, like our music galleries in ball-rooms. It is one mass of mirrors, intermixed with green foil, inlaid with gilt wooden partitions and numbers of English cut-glass chandeliers. The decorations were covered, to save them as well as their master. To the fête in the honour of this tutelary divinity, the Resident was always invited, and the Peshwa did not himself do the honours, as he was also a visitor to his long-nosed patron. I saw here an English clock which was found going well, in the palace ; several large English books of

> fine engravings, and the remains of a very large orrery nearly destroyed. There was, besides, a native map, but I imagine Goklah must have a better one, to have so long escaped our pursuing army."

This was perhaps the last description of the Palace that had been written while the building existed intact, for, in June 1818, the Peshwa abdicated his Gadi or throne to Sir John Malcolm and went to reside at Bithur near Cawnpur as a political prisoner of the British Government.

Exactly ten years after this event the whole Palace was completely burnt down by a great fire on the 27th February 1827, which lasted for seven days, and except the heavy rampart, strong gateways and buried foundations and ruins that still bear witness to the rise and fall of a mighty Empire, nothing of this majestic and magnificent building has been saved from the cruel hand of Time. It is only the Nagarkhana or music gallery on the top of the Delhi gate which once sang loudly the glories of the great Peshwas, now seen mourning in silence.

II.

PARVATI AND ITS TEMPLES.

PARVATI is a small hill situated to the south-west of the historic town of Poona. It is about 500 yards from the city limits and about $3\frac{1}{2}$ miles from the Poona Post Office. It has become famous on account of the temples which were built by the third Peshwa Balaji Bajirao (1740-1761). Before that, it had no importance and was included in a small hamlet called Parvati which was under Poona since the Nizamshahi kingdom. It is mentioned in an old document that it was given in *inam* to a Brahman named Mahadbhat *bin* Mudgalbhat Purandare and was continued to him by the celebrated Malik Ambar, as well as Shahaji and Shivaji. After the death of Dadaji Kondadev, in 1647, the title of the Brahman was questioned and he was stopped from enjoying the revenue of the village. Whereupon the Brahmin made a complaint to Shivaji, who, on inquiry, restored the village of Parvati to Purandare. It is well-known in Maratha history that the descendants of this Purandare family afterwards helped Balaji

POONA IN 1800.

Vishwanath, the first Peshwa, in his early days of adversity, and subsequently carved out their own fortune along with him. In 1714 when Balaji Vishwanath was invested with the office of Peshwa, Ambaji Trimbak was made his Mutalik or Dewan and given a Saranjam of Rs. 65,000. His descendants are still enjoying the Jahagir and are styled as first class Sardars of the Deccan. The grandson of Balaji Vishwanath took a fancy for the Parvati Hill, built some beautiful temples and buildings, and turned it into a picturesque and romantic place.

The story goes that Kashibai, mother of Balaji Bajirao Peshwa, suffered from sore-feet and came to reside in the Mastani Garden for change. All possible efforts were made to cure her but to no purpose. She then prayed to the hill goddess Parvatai (Bhawani) to restore her to health and her ailments immediately stopped. The image of the goddess was then in a neglected condition and the Peshwa's mother asked her dutiful son to build a temple in honour of the goddess Parvati and Balaji Bajirao complied with her wishes. The author of the Peshwa's Bakhar gives another tale. He says that Balaji Bajirao built a temple of Shiva in honour of Raja Shahu to perpetuate his memory. Whatever may be the true version,

Parvati temples were built by the third Peshwa, Balaji Bajirao, whose name has been associated with the hill in a manner worthy of his illustrious fame.

Balaji Bajirao selected a good site on the summit of the hill and commenced a building of stone work in 1748. From the authority of state records it is evident that the following idols were placed with religious ceremonies in the temple on the 11th April 1749:—

1. Devadeveshwar (*Ban.*)
2. Mahadeo of silver with two golden images—one Ganpati on its right lap and the other Parvati on its left lap.
3. Ganpati of stone.
4. Parvati—the original idol of the hill goddess which was already there.

The religious ceremonies and the dinners in connection with them were celebrated continuously for four days from Friday 7th April to 10th April by the Peshwa and Rs. 4,320 were spent on that account. The silver idol of Mahadeo weighed 6,737½ rupees and the two golden images of Ganpati and Parvati weighed tolas 686 and 1,245 respectively.

The Peshwa Balaji regularly rode every morning to Parvati and spent hours in enjoying the scenery there, and in taking athletic exercises. Later on, he became so deeply devoted to the gods that on every Ekadashi day he worshipped the idols himself. He also appointed several Brahmans to perform the religious worship of Devadeveshwar. In 1760 he guilded spires of the temples with gold weighing 1,020 tolas. In 1763 when the Moguls destroyed the town of Poona, the idols in the Parvati temples were removed elsewhere and they were again brought there and replaced with religious ceremonies. In the centre lies the chief temple which is dedicated to Devadeveshwar, another name for Shiva. It is a handsome building with imposing gateway built after Hindu style with a spire and guilt top. At every corner of the temple are small domed shrines dedicated to the Sun, Ganesh, Parvati, and Vishnu. In front of the chief God there is a carved stone bull covered by a stone canopy. In a separate enclosure to the west of the main temple are two more temples dedicated to Kartik-swami and Vishnu. The architecture of these temples is not particularly remarkable but the effect of grouping adds immensely to the general view.

In 1755 the Peshwa Balaji Bajirao built on the hill private quarters for change and recreation and he often visited them. They are still known as the 'Wada' or Palace. He was so much heart broken by the crushing defeat of Panipat that he was removed to Parvati by his ministers, Konher Trimbak Ekbote and Krishnarao Parasnis, for change where he died in 1761. His son, Madhavrao I, followed in his footsteps and showed great regard for his father's dearly loved hill. On the 21st February 1766 he established the Shivapanchayatan or the five smaller gods in the main temple of Devadeveshwar and continued all the grants to the temple. Nana Phadnavis prayed to the goddess Parvatai that if a son was born to Narayanrao's widow Gangabai his thread ceremony would be performed on the Parvati hill. The goddess listened to his prayers and blessed the lady with a son, and Nana in order to fulfil his vow celebrated the thread ceremony of the young Peshwa on Parvati in 1779. On this occasion valuable presents were given to the temples and considerable charities were distributed at Parvati. The young Peshwa Sawai Madhavrao, too, like his grandfather, showed great liking for the hill and took frequent rides there; his chief attraction being the menagerie which was located at the foot of the hill. Bajirao II, the last Peshwa, commenced to build a storeyed palace here, but his stars being unfavourable he left every thing in chaos and ruin. The palace begun by him was never finished and the completed parts of it were destroyed by lightning in 1816. In 1791 in the reign of Sawai Madhavrao, lightning had struck the temple of Kartik Swami which was considered a bad omen by Brahmans and a Shanti (propitiating) ceremony was performed to appease the God! But in 1816 all the elements being enraged against the last Peshwa he could not win the blessings of Parvati. It is said that he witnessed the battle of Kirkee from a window in the northern wall in the main temple but he was terrified and ran away when he heard the thundering sounds of cannon.

The temples of Parvati are built at a height of 216 feet from the base, but being situated on a fortified eminence they present a most charming and magnificent view. The ascent is by a flight of very wide and long stone-steps numbering about a hundred. The steps are so built that elephants could ascend the hill easily. Palanquins and elephants were the usual conveyances for royalties in those days but the practice of utilising them has since disappeared. The last ascent that was made on an elephant was on the occasion of the visit of H. R. H. the Prince of Wales to Poona in 1877, when the huge animal slipped and nearly fell with the Prince. The view from the Nagarkhana is one of the most beautiful scenes that can possibly be presented to the eye. The spectator is bewildered, as it were, by the surrounding scenery. It bursts upon his sight so suddenly and so pleasingly, that he feels puzzled on which side to fix his attention. Beauty meets the eye from every point, green of every shade, brilliant and glittering. It was from this place that the Peshwa used to see the fire-works which were played in the tank below. Parvati is indeed an ornament to the Maratha capital and Poona is justly proud of her temples and their builders.

At the foot of the Parvati hill, a high enclosure of masonry was built by the Peshwa Balaji Bajirao for distributing alms in the month of Shrawan to Brahmans from all parts of the Deccan, Berar, Carnatic and Hindustan proper, according to the sanctity, moral character and learning of the individual. It was known as *Ramana* or gathering of Brahmans which was held annually like a religious fair at the Parvati hill. This institution was started by Bajirao I, in Poona after his victory over Trimbakrao Dabhade in 1731. In 1736 the total amount of Dakshina was Rs. 16,354 only, but it gradually rose to lacs and the following figures show how the institution grew along with the prosperity of the Peshwas :—

		Rs.
Year A. D. 1737	.. ..	49,073
,, ,, 1749	.. ..	1,23,530

			Rs.
Year A. D.	1752	.. ..	6,28,353
„ „	1753	.. ..	2,06,019
„ „	1762	.. ..	11,898
„ „	1765	.. ..	1,32,043
„ „	1768	.. ..	2,88,745
„ „	1776	.. ..	5,05,128
„ „	1788	.. ..	2,18,630
„ „	1789	.. ..	2,25,354

These figures are interesting as they throw a light on the social and material progress of the country. It is significant to note that in 1762 the figure of the Dakshina was reduced to a few thousands owing to the terrible havoc wrought in Maharashtra by the battle of Panipat in 1761. It again rose to its normal condition as the country regained peace and prosperity. The highest amount of Dakshina during the reign of Sawai Madhavrao was about 5 lacs. The result of this munificence brought credit to Poona as a city of learning and attracted learned men from all parts of India. Brahmans from Shringeri, Conjivaram, Seringapatam, Kumbhakonam, Tanjore, Ram-eshwar in the south, and Benares, Kanoj, Gwalior, Muttra in the north, attended the annual gathering and represented all branches of religious and other learning. Amongst them were Vaidiks, Grammarians, Astrologers, Pandits, Poets, Vedantists, Logicians, Ascetics and also Doctors. They were examined by the learned Shastris of Poona, namely Ram Shastri Prabhune, Bal Shastri, Ayya Shastri, and Kashinath Shastri and were paid the Dakshina according to their proficiency, the highest amount being Rs. 1,000. The learned men were received and paid in the Palace according to their tested merits and others in the *Ramana* near Parvati with food. There were four doors to the compound and the Peshwa, Nana Phadnavis, Ram Shastri, Amritrao, and other officers were seated at every door with proper guards for distributing money. It was rather a heavy task but with proper arrangement of the Police and Military it passed off smoothly and peacefully. The Dakshina or annual gathering of Brahmans at Parvati for receiving alms had become an interesting spectacle in Poona, and many Europeans from the Residency visited the scene out of curiosity. Captain Moor visited Parvati in 1797 and gives a most interesting graphic account of the Dakshina ceremony. He writes :—

"Parvati, generally called Parbaty, is a hill of considerable height at the southern end of the city of Poona ; on the summit of which is a handsome, but not very elegant temple in honour of Parvati, consort of Mahadeva. It is a very respectable temple, and much resorted to ; and when lighted up on great occasions, it shows well ; and from its top is a fine view of the city and environs. On the annual ceremony of Datchna, or alms-giving, great sums are given away at Parbaty. To this temple Brahmans come to share the loaves and fishes from considerable distances ; it would not be worth the pains for the majority to come so far merely for what they get here ; but as a gift on this day tells ten fold of an ordinary alms, others, as well as the Peshwa, make presents to some Brahmans, as do generous people on the road to and from this meritorious pilgrimage. The whole month is indeed, very fit for the benefit of hospitality and alms-giving, so that the travelling Brahmans are fed, etc., all the way to Poona and home. Some come from Surat, Panderpoor, and other more distant places ; and it is confidently said, that forty thousand have been known to assemble on this occasion at Parbaty.

"It is customary, on a few preceding days, for the Peshwa and other great men, to entertain Brahmans of eminence and to make them presents ; and these favoured and learned persons do not crowd with the mob, if we may so designate so holy a congress, to Parvati. The Peshwa, it is said, gives some fifty, some a hundred, and even so far as a thousand rupees, according, as my learned informant tells me, to their virtue and knowledge ; but it is not likely that any examination or scrutiny can take place, or that the bounty can be bestowed otherwise than by favour and interest, tempered, perhaps, by the reputation or appearance of the receiver.

"About Parvati are some enclosures ; one square field has a high wall all about it, with four entrances through double gates. It is not usual for any but Brahmans to be admitted on the day of the Datchna ; but, desirous of seeing what was going forward, Captain Gardner and I, by the exercise of a little civility and patience, were let in, but not our attendants, as no Brahman was among them.

"It appeared that at three of the four entrances Brahmans were admitted and money given ; and it was our intention to have observed them all ; but, soon after our entrance, Amritrao, the Peshwa's elder brother by adoption, who was superintending one of the gates, hearing there were gentlemen of the English Residency in the field, sent to invite us to visit him, an honour which we could not, of course, decline ; and he detained us in conversation so long, that it was necessary to proceed immediately home, on account of the approaching night.

" At this gate, where we heard the operation of weighing and moving money, stood a cauldron of red liquid from which a man, dipping his hand in, marked every candidate on some part of his garment, or, in default of garment, on his skin with its expanded impression, and admitted him. It was now six in the evening, and the field was not half full—some thousands were waiting outside ; but I should not, at a round guess, suppose that the field would contain many more than twenty thousand ; to get money, however, a Brahman will make himself very small. We understand that until ten at night Brahmans were admitted ; indeed, I suppose, no candidate is excluded. They are kept in the field until all are collected ; but it is not clear to me whether the money is given at the entrance or exit : at any rate it is expedient to keep them all together, or a cunning one might get two shares. If paid at entering, I see no use for the mark of the red hand ; which would avail, if all were marked at entering, kept until the whole were collected, and, on showing the mark, paid, and let out. We observed no paying where we entered, and concluded that the money was given at quitting the field.

"The usual dole I learned was from three to ten rupees, and I believe caprice or pleasure is the chief guide as to the amount. One pleasant jolly looking fellow, who was waiting with us on the outside, said he expected to get five, seven, or ten rupees ; but I could not gather from him what might ensure him a high share, or confine him to a low one : he said, indeed, that it was all fortune or fate. He had come from Surat ; and on being asked how he found his account in coming so far on so slender an expectancy, he said he had nothing profitable to do at home, and was fed all the way out and home, received other hospitalities and alms on the road, and visited and met his friends, relations and acquaintances ; and paid his devotions also at other holy places near his route, which he contrived to make very pleasant by taking his own time, and farther, that there was reputation, as well as other benefits, allied to this fort of pilgrimage. He was gratified at my wishing, on taking leave, that he might this year receive a sum of rupees commensurate rather with his merit than his fortune, which I could not doubt would be three hundred at least. He had said that last year his fate produced him but three rupees; this he volunteered, as I avoided putting the question, inferring, from his attributing a large sum to fortune, that his acquisition was but small.

"The arrangement at the gate we understood to be this: the Peshwa at one; Amritrao, Chimna Appa (the Peshwa's younger brother) and Nana, at the other three. Dowlutrao Sindia was likewise there, and we saw him go away on horseback about five o'clock. An immense crowd of people were assembled about Parbaty. The donations this year (1797) were greater than usual: Bajirao, (the Peshwa) perhaps had mind to be prodigal, to gain popularity; but Nana was said to have disapproved of it at such a time. The Peshwa was understood to have given away five Lakhs (5,00,000) of rupees: about sixty-two thousand pounds.

> " I note as rather an extraordinary thing, that a man, not, I think, a Brahman, who had been instrumental in obtaining us admission refused to accept a rupee in return. I please myself by thinking he was not the man, nor our broad-faced friend of Surat, who took my topaz-pin ; for some one had the address, while I was in the crowd, to convey a very handsome one from my shirt."

During the reign of Bajirao II, the institution of Dakshina was continued; the amount grew to eight to ten lacs, but it was distributed indiscriminately to all Brahmans reserving only a portion as a reward for learning. After the overthrow of the Peshwa's rule in 1818, the British Government discontinued the public distribution of Dakshina at Parvati, but appreciating the object of the charity in its true sense allotted a special allowance for the encouragement of learning. That enlightened and wise statesman, Sir Mount-Stuart Elphinstone, who viewed this institution in its true aspect wrote in 1821 : " The Dakshina was expressly designed to encourage learning. It formerly amounted to eight or ten lacs of rupees and though Bajirao reduced the expenses, he still gave a small sum to each of 50,000 Brahmans, besides large prizes to all who distinguished themselves by their learning.

Both he and all his Sardars and Ministers employed many learned Brahmans in various offices connected with the Hindu ritual ; and all on a religious principle, allowed stipends and grants of land to many others for whose services they had no call. Add to this that learning was a certain title to the countenance of the great and to the respect of the people and we may estimate the incentives to the acquisition of it which were destroyed by our conquest. It is true that his encouragement may not have been judiciously directed, but the effects of it on the whole were beneficial, and such as I cannot but think that it is still desirable to preserve. A class of men was maintained whose time was devoted to the cultivation of their understanding ; their learning may have been obscure and degenerate, but still it bore some affinity to real science into which it might in time have been improved. They were not perhaps much inferior to those monks among whom the seeds of European learning were long kept alive ; and their extinctions, if it did not occasion the loss of much present wisdom, would have cut off all hope for the future."

It may be mentioned that the Dakshina grant specially sanctioned by Sir Mount-Stuart Elphinstone was afterwards utilized in establishing a Sanskrit Pathshala and scholarships which popularized the study of Sanskrit literature and philosophy among all classes of students, and the present Dakshina fellowships and the Dakshina Prize Fund are the last remnants of that famous institution.

SIR CHARLES MALET, RESIDENT AT POONA (1786-1796).

III.

THE SANGAM OR THE BRITISH RESIDENCY AT POONA.

THE Sangam, now known as the Judge's Bungalow at Poona, is a place of great historical interest. The meaning of the word Sangam is a confluence of two rivers. This site Sir Charles Malet, the first British Resident, selected and built on it a house in 1787, which afterwards attained a great importance in the political history of Poona. It is therefore necessary to give a short account of the place as well as its distinguished residents.

James Douglas has justly observed in his Book of Bombay that the Malet family within a hundred years gave to diplomacy, three individuals of note in direct succession. The first in this notable series was Charles Warre Malet who rose to the responsible position of the Resident at the Peshwa's Court at Poona in 1786. He came to India in 1770 and accepted a writership in the civil department under the East India Company. By his talents and activity he soon rose to distinction and was appointed Resident at Cambay in

1774. He then became Private Secretary to the Governor of Bombay and was appointed British Resident at Poona in 1786. The treaty of Salbai in 1782 closed the first Maratha War and a permanent friendship was assured between the Marathas and the English; but the formidable activities of the rival powers such as the French, the Portuguese, Tipu Sultan of Mysore, and the Nizam impressed upon the English the idea of keeping a permanent Resident at Poona. The English had on previous occasions sent envoys to Poona such as Captain Gordon, Major Price, Mr. Mostyn, Colonel Upton and others on diplomatic missions, but now they saw the necessity of having a permanent representative at Poona and solicited the permission of the Maratha Government for the purpose. After some hesitation and discussion Nana Phadnavis was compelled to accede to their request, and the acting Governor-General Mr. Macpherson at once selected Charles Warre Malet to take up that diplomatic and responsible position. By the treaty of Salbai Mahadji Sindia was considered to be the mutual guarantee for the perpetual and invariable adherence of both parties to the terms of the treaty and it was therefore necessary to secure his consent to this new proposal. Malet therefore proceeded to Northern India to meet Mahadji

Sindia. After a long and tedious journey he reached Muttra and met the Maratha intermediary on the 20th March 1785. Mahadji was naturally reluctant to accept such a proposal by which his own influence was to be shaken. Nevertheless Malet with the help of Mr. Anderson, the English envoy at Sindia's Court, succeeded in prevailing upon Mahadji to signify his assent to this proposal which had already been accepted by the Peshwa. Thus having gained his object Malet proceeded to Calcutta to see the acting Governor-General Mr. Macpherson, who issued his orders appointing him British Resident at Poona. Malet, who had upto now been a subordinate of the Bombay Government was appointed as a representative of the Calcutta Government and was placed under their control and guidance. He was styled in all correspondence as *Vakil nisbat Kalkattekar*, *i.e.*, Envoy on behalf of the Calcutta Government.

From Calcutta Malet went to Bombay in January 1786 and thence proceeded to Poona to take charge of the newly created Residency at Poona. Nana Phadnavis, the Chief Minister of Poona Durbar, had gone to the Carnatic on the expedition against Tipu. He therefore deputed Bahiro Raghunath Mehendale to receive the new Resident and to make suitable arrangements for him at Poona. Bahiro Raghunath who was called

'Bahiro Pandit' in the English correspondence was a trusted officer of the Peshwa's Court, who acted as Nana's vakil with the Resident and discussed state matters on behalf of his master as long as Malet was at Poona. He possessed attractive manners and unusual tact and cultivated great friendship with the Resident.

Malet arrived in Poona on the 3rd March 1786 and was well received by Bahiro Raghunath on behalf of the Poona Durbar. He had a large retinue with him including six European officers. Of these three were entitled to the honour of being carried in palanquins. He had also 35 horses, 200 guards, 100 followers, 50 hamals and kamathis, 75 dooly bearers, 425 coolies, 2 elephants and 5 palanquins, besides one large tent, two small tents and three big rahutees and several small rahutees. In his suite was a Mahomedan lady friend of Malet who rode in a palanquin.

According to the state formalities and ceremonials, there was considerable discussion on the subject of Malet's reception, but it was decided that he should be treated by the Peshwa's Government with the same dignity and courtesy which were shown to former British ambassadors, Mr. Mostyn and Colonel Upton. Bahiropant reported full particulars of the reception to Nana

Phadnavis. From his report it appears that Malet was received by the Peshwa's representative at Ganesh Khind whence he was taken to the Gaikwad's mansion which was selected for his residence. Malet stayed there with a few select persons of his suite, and the whole retinue was kept in a garden near Parvati. He afterwards pitched his tents opposite Parvati near Anandrao Jivaji's garden and himself lived there for some time.

On his arrival in Poona, Malet wanted to pay a state visit to the Peshwa and offer him several presents which he had specially brought. Amongst them was a large griffin bird (presumably an ostrich) from Abyssinia, four feet high ; but unfortunately it died in its cage below the Ghauts, and its body was brought to Poona. Malet obtained leave to see the Peshwa, but according to the old custom it was decided to give him the same reception which was given to the English ambassadors on former occasion. Malet was displeased with this decision. He contended that English envoys who had visited Poona in the past represented the Bombay Government, while he had now come on behalf of the Calcutta Government and he ought to be received with the same honours and presented with an elephant as was done by the Mogul Emperor or Mahadji Sindia. After some unpleasant discussion Malet was accorded an interview by the Peshwa and the question of presenting an elephant was altogether dropped.

In 1786 Malet made his permanent residence at Poona and requested the Peshwa to allot him a piece of ground for building a bungalow for himself and his staff outside the town. He selected the picturesque site near the Sangam which was afterwards approved and sanctioned by the Peshwa's Government. It appears that a plot of ground was given to Malet near Bibi Saidani's Darga or shrine near the Sangam, and the first house that was built there for the Residency was on the spot where the Judge's Office is situated at present. This place Malet soon developed into a splendid park with a beautiful building in the centre. He lived in the rich style that befitted his position, and entertained the Peshwa and his courtiers at his house. Captain Moor describes his residence in 1791 in the following terms:—

"The residence of Sir Charles Malet is known by the name of the Sungum, being situated, as the word denotes, at the confluence of two rivers the Moota and the Moola.. .. .. Sir Charles' former residence was in the city, but not being a pleasant situation, he was permitted to build habitations on this spot, which until that time had no buildings of any kind, save an old neglected pagoda in ruins, still remaining in the gardens, a contrast to the neatness of the buildings erected at a great expense by him, and the gentlemen of his suite. The Sungum is a little town quite detached from the city, being divided from it by the Moota, and inhabited entirely by the gentlemen, their attendants, and two companies of sepoys, stationed here as the Resident's honorary guard. Sir Charles' garden is watered by both rivers, by means of aqueducts: it produces all the fruits and vegetables of this country; here is an excellent vineyard: apple and peach trees thrive well, and promise to be a great acquisition to the horticulture of these parts. Stately cypress and other ornamental trees, contribute to make this a charming retreat, and we readily declare, that with the advantages of society and situation, the Sungum is the most enviable residence we ever saw in India. Sir Charles' stud is elegant, consisting of forty or fifty noble animals from Arabia, Persia, &c. Several elephants on state visits compose part of the retinue. This show is requisite at Eastern Courts, where there is always considerable pomp, and it is necessary for ambassadors to assume an appearance of ceremonious dignity."

Malet having settled at Poona rendered valuable diplomatic services to the East India Company. In those days Tipu had become very powerful and his progress was dreaded by the Marathas as well as the English. It was therefore thought necessary to crush his constantly growing strength by leading a joint expedition against him. Malet succeeded in negotiating a triple alliance between the Marathas, the English and the Nizam. He exhibited great diplomatic genius and tact in bringing about this important treaty, which was signed by the Peshwa in the Ganpati Rang-mahal on the 1st June 1790. By this agreement the armies of the three great powers combined together and led a successful expedition against Tipu. Lord Cornwalis commanded the English army, while Secunderjah, the son of the Nizam, and his Minister, Mir Alam, commanded the Nizam's forces; and Parashuram Bhao Patwardhan and Haripant Phadke were at the head of the Maratha armies. All these allied forces invaded Tipu and conquered half of his country, which was afterwards divided amongst the three powers. The political services rendered by Malet in this respect were highly appreciated by the British Government who created him a Baronet on 24th February 1791.

Sir Charles Malet was a very popular person in Poona society. He not only promoted his nation's political and commercial interests but also introduced European arts, science, and medicine into the Maratha society. The contact and influence of such an accomplished and amiable person proved beneficial in many ways. It was Malet who introduced the famous artist Mr. James Wales to the Peshwa's Court who sketched several important personages in Poona. Wales came to Poona in 1790 and lived there till his death in 1795. His portraits of the Peshwa Sawai Madhavrao, Nana Phadnavis and Mahadji Sindia are still in existence. Malet induced the Peshwa to establish a school of drawing in his palace and the artist Wales was selected to be the superintendent in charge of the school. He taught several Indian pupils amongst whom Gangaram Tambat became very proficient. He made drawings of the Ellora or Verul caves, which were presented to Sir John Shore, the Governor-General, in 1794.

Drs. Crusoe and Findlay, the Residency Surgeons, contributed to the spread of English medical treatment and many persons of rank and distinction took English medicines prescribed by these skilful doctors regardless of any religious scruples.

Sir Charles Malet and his friends presented several telescopes, globes and many other appliances of English science to the Peshwa who was exceedingly charmed with them. It is on record that Dr. Findlay gave lessons to the Peshwa in astronomy and geography and received handsome rewards from him.

The interest of Malet's career at Poona lay more in the social relations which he cultivated with all the people in Poona from the Peshwa down to the lowest clerk, and his success was mainly due to his intimate knowledge of oriental manners and customs, and his genial good nature and free intercourse with the people. He regularly attended Ganpati festivals in the Peshwa's palace and at the houses of several noblemen, and was always present at their marriage and thread ceremonies. In fact, he endeared himself to every one in Poona and became a great social success.

Malet was present in Poona till 1795. He was extremely sorry at the sad death of the Peshwa Sawai Madavrao and wrote to Nana Phadnavis a touching letter of condolence. When Bajirao II succeeded to the Gadi, Malet became an equally great friend of the new Peshwa. Malet's intimate relations with the Maratha Court disclosed to him the faults and weaknesses of the Maratha people and their government. When he accompanied the Maratha armies in their expedition against

NURUDDIN HUSSEINKHAN, RESIDENCY VAKIL WITH THE PESHWA.

the Nizam in 1795, he saw the utter want of discipline in them and observed in one of his dispatches that such a disorganized army could be vanquished in no time by a small but well disciplined force. I need not mention how this prophesy came true.

Sir Charles Malet was a keen observer of men and things and had selected the best men for his service. Syed Nuruddin Hussein Khan was his diplomatic agent in the Poona Durbar and used to assist him in his political business. This gentleman was a great Persian scholar and was highly spoken of by Major Price.—"He (Sir Charles Malet) had in his suit a Mogul Khan or Nobleman, once high in station in the Court of Delhi, and of the very highest attainments in Persian literature; several of the sons of this nobleman were also in Sir Charles' suite. He had, in particular, been the friend and associate of the celebrated Gazhi-ud-din, celebrated perhaps, as much for his crimes as for his abilities as a statesman. From his habits of constant personal communication with this old nobleman Sir Charles Malet had become the most practical Persian scholar I have ever met." It is a well known fact that Sir Charles was a great Persian scholar and that he had collected an excellent Persian library of most valuable illuminated manuscripts which he afterwards presented to the Royal Asiatic Society of London.

It is interesting to note that Sir Charles Malet visited the Mahableshwar Hills in November 1791 in company with the Peshwa, and justly claims the credit of being the first European discoverer of that charming place. Sir Charles left the Poona Residency in 1796 and was promoted to the membership of the Council in Bombay where he acted as Governor for some time. He kept his friendly relations with the Peshwa's Court and had a regular correspondence with the Peshwa and Nana Phadnavis. He did not remain long in Bombay. Having put in arduous and meritorious service for 27 years he retired and left for England in March 1797. Befoie leaving the Indian shores for good, he paid his last visit to Poona on the 21st February 1797, when the Peshwa Bajirao presented him with a farewell dress of honour, and sent with him a friendly letter and costly presents to the King of England.

Sir Charles Malet married Lady Susan, the daughter of the artist, Wales. By her he had eight sons, the eldest Sir Alexander Malet succeeded to his father's title and was English Ambassador at Berlin from 1856 to 1866. Another son, Sir Arthur Malet, was a member at the

Bombay Council, and the third son, Mr. Hugh Malet was a Bombay Civilian, who, while Collector at Thana, discovered the Matheran Hills. Sir Charles Malet died at Wilbury House in 1815. He was figuratively called the "Maker of Sangam" meaning the connecting link of the East and the West.

After Sir Charles Malet left the Poona Residency, his Assistant Mr. Uhthoff, a man of practical common sense, acted as Resident for some time. In 1798 Lt.-Col. William Palmer came to Poona and took charge of the Poona Residency. He had served in various capacities in Bengal and had become famous in diplomatic circles. He was Military Secretary to Warren Hastings for several years and became Resident of Lucknow in 1782. On account of his high merits and political knowledge he was specially selected as Resident to Mahadji Sindia's Court where he earned a considerable reputation and also gained a deep insight into Maratha affairs. From Sindia's Court he was transferred to the Poona Residency where he served from 1798 to 1801—a period full of trouble and confusion. He calmly watched the events that took place in the Poona Court and strictly followed the policy of non-intervention. His despatches are very wise and sober. He was a great admirer of Nana Phadnavis and was present in Poona when that renowned Statesman died in 1800. While reporting his death to Government he remarked in his despatch, that "with Nana departed all the wisdom and moderation of the Maratha Government." In 1801 Sir Barry Close was appointed Resident at Poona and Col. Palmer was sent on Military duty. He afterwards commanded at Monghyr and died at Burhampur May 20, 1814.

Sir Barry Close, the third Resident at Poona, entered the army in 1772, and the following year joined one of the batallions of the Indian European Regiment, and served with the corps throughout the early Mysore wars. After filling many high and important situations he became Adjutant-General of the Madras Army, and as such performed most distinguished services in the last war against Tipu Sultan, and was present at the siege and capture of Seringapatam in 1799. He was subsequently appointed by the Marquis Wellesley, on account of his eminent talents and integrity, as well as his knowledge of the language, manners and customs of the natives, Resident at Mysore. In 1800 the Hon'ble Court of Directors, in testimony of their high sense of his services, presented him with a sword worth three hundred guineas. He rendered most valuable services in establishing peace and good government at Mysore, and his memory was perpetuated there by calling a village after his name "Close-peth" which is still a flourishing town in the Mysore State. He was appointed Resident at Poona in 1801 and held that office till 1810. While at Poona he negotiated the famous treaty of Bassein with the last Peshwa Bajirao on the 31st December 1802. He was a consumate politician and a sober thinker, and those who saw and knew him have expressed a high opinion of him. Sir James Mackintosh who met him in Poona in 1808 writes:—"I am as much struck as I was at first by the character of Colonel Close. He is without accomplishment of show, plain, cautious, and with a degree of mildness, that forms a singular contrast with the firmness, and even sternness, which he has shown on trying occasions. He has a calm understanding, wholly employed in practice, united to a strength of a nerve, which qualifies him equally for a cautious and vigorous policy. He is a very superior man, who might easily pass among common observers for a very common man." When he died Sir Mount Stuart Elphinstone wrote in one of his letters:—"I doubt whether such an assembly of manly virtues remains behind him. A strong, erect and hardy frame, a clear head and vigorous understanding, fixed principles, unshaken courage, contempt for pomp and pleasure, entire devotion to the public service, formed the character of Sir Barry Close—a character one would rather think imagined in ancient Rome, than met with in our age and nation."

Colonel Close kept up friendly relations with the Poona Durbar and observed oriental etiquette and manners. In his time the Poona Residency was a charming place. "His gardens" wrote Lord Valentia, "are on the banks of the Moota where it joins the Moola, and forms the Moota-Moola river. It is a charming spot adorned with cypress and fruit trees. At the point a very handsome bungalow is erected, where breakfast and dinner were served; at one end is a billiard table for the idlers. The Colonel keeps a very excellent table; beef, however, out of respect to the prejudices of the natives is never used. Holkar when here, had so little control over the Pathan troops, that the sacred animal was frequently slaughtered." The large house or the bungalow which was built at the Residency owed its existence to Colonel Close who with the help of the Peshwa Bajirao got it erected in commemoration of the Maratha War in 1804. Colonel Close retired in 1810 and went to England when the Government of Madras expressed their appreciation of his eminent and distinguished services. He died in 1813. The

Court of Directors sent to India a splendid monument to his memory in 1818, which was erected in St. Mary's Church, Fort St. George, Madras.

Mr. Elphinstone who was in 1801, an assistant to Sir Barry Close, succeeded him at the Poona Residency in 1810. His life is full of varied interest but it is not possible here to give it in detail. At an early age he entered the service of the East India Company and after serving in various capacities he came to Poona in 1801. At the time the Peshwa Bajirao was on the throne and the Maratha confederacy had greatly declined. Hostilities soon arose between its chief members, Sindia and Holker. War was declared against Sindia and his friend the Raja of Nagpur. General Wellesley took the field in person and young Elphinstone was attached to his staff. At the battle of Assaye, 23rd September 1803, Elphinstone was by the General's side and his letters contain an animated picture of the action. By the treaty of Surji Anjangaon peace was concluded with the Marathas, and on the recommendation of General Wellesley, Elphinstone was appointed in 1804 to the important post of the Resident at Nagpur, which he held till 1808. Wellesley paid a high compliment to Elphinstone for his conspicuous services and merits in the campaign, and remarked in one of his despatches that he (Elphinstone) had mistaken his profession and ought to have been a soldier! In 1808 Elphinstone was appointed Ambassador to the Afghan Court of Cabul, with a view to establish English influence there. On his return from the Cabul mission he was appointed Resident at Poona in 1810.

The signal services of Elphinstone at Poona are conspicuous in history. The Peshwa Bajirao was a weak and vicious ruler and was under evil influence. In 1815 he connived at the murder of Gangadhar Shastri, an envoy from Baroda, which made Elphinstone interfere. He demanded the dismissal of Trimbakji, a favourite of the Peshwa, who was said to be the real culprit. The Peshwa shuffled and a political struggle commenced between the Poona Durbar and the English. Elphinstone suspected the fidelity of the Peshwa and demanded a new treaty which the Peshwa signed on 10th May 1816; but he continued to intrigue against British Government and increase his forces. The storm soon broke. The Peshwa began to hem in the Residency and Elphinstone ordered up reinforcement for its defence. The Peshwa's army attacked the Residency on the 5th November 1817. Elphinstone was already aware of the danger and a few hours previous to the attack he evacuated the Residency and retired to the camp at Kirkee. The Marathas fell upon the abandoned Residency which was burned with all that it contained, including Elphinstone's beloved books and the whole of his private property. About sunset the English army under Col. Burr gallantly fought with the Maratha forces and utterly routed them. In this battle the Peshwa's Second-in-Command, Moro Dikshit, fell, and the Peshwa himself ran away. The city was captured by the English and the British Flag was hoisted on the Peshwa's Palace.

The battle of Kirkee gave a death-blow to the Maratha power and the events that followed it completed the annexation of the Peshwa's territories. Elphinstone took charge of the conquered country and devoted all his talents and energy in establishing tranquillity and peace and in organizing a civil government. Though the task was most arduous and difficult, Elphinstone achieved it with wonderful success. He left his mark as a wise, just and generous administrator and his illustrious name is still held in reverence and honour in the Deccan. In 1819 he was raised to the Governorship of Bombay, where he earned great success and popularity. He retired in 1827 and died on the 20th November 1859 at Hoodhook, his residence in Scotland.

The Sangam or the Residency was very much improved by Elphinstone. It included the adjoining grounds of the present Science College and the English Burial Ground close to the Sangam Lodge. The Resident's Quarters contained five bungalows and many out houses for the body-guards and sentries. The present building is an altogether modern structure built on the ruins of the old Residency. It still possesses a peculiar interest on account of its historical association and picturesque scenery and is included in the list of ancient monuments of Poona.

MAHADJI SINDIA, GREAT MARATHA WARRIOR AND STATESMAN.

IV.

SINDIA'S CHHATRI.

SINDIA'S Chhatri or tomb is an object of great historical interest in Poona. It lies on the left bank of a stream, known as Bahiroba's Stream, in the south-east corner of Wanavdi, a village three miles from Poona. Here the great Mahadji Sindia was cremated after his death on the 12th February 1794. To mark the site of the funeral pyre, which is considered very sacred by Hindus, a Chhatri or tomb has been built by H. H. the Maharaja of Gwalior. Till recently, there was no proper building but a small hamlet of a few houses surrounded by a wall, known as 'Sindia's Chhatri,' in which were situated two small shrines of Maruti and Mahadeo. This little hamlet came into existence after the death of Mahadji Sindia. His adopted son and heir, Dowlatrao Sindia, requested the Peshwa Sawai Madhavrao to grant him a piece of ground for the tomb of his father near the place, and orders were accordingly issued on the 5th of September 1795; but it appears that Dowlatrao Sindia only commenced the building and left it unfinished. In 1805 Sir James Mackintosh paid a visit to this place, which he describes in his diary as follows:—

> "On the way to the camp we visited a monument which had been begun to be erected to Mahadji Scindia, but which was suspended by the civil war, and is probably now relinquished for ever. The masonry was admirable, and the work promised to be very handsome. Near the bottom was a cornice of *fleurs de lys*, which none of us could explain. Pretty near this monument is a sorry hut where the ashes of this powerful chieftain were deposited for a time and where they may now lie long undisturbed. It is a small pagoda where, in the usual place of the principal Deity, is a picture of Scindia by Zoffany, very like that in the Government house at Bombay. Before the picture, lights are kept constantly burning, and offerings daily made by an old servant of the Maharajah, whose fidelity rather pleased me, even though I was told that this little pagoda was endowed with lands, which yielded a small income, sufficient for the worship and the priest. This portrait, by Zoffany, is

> probably the only work of European art which is now the object of adoration; it has obtained one honour refused to the 'Transfiguration' itself."

From this evidence it is pretty clear that the civil war and chaos which followed the death of Mahadji Sindia in Poona, came in the way of the building, and the fine work of the monument undertaken by Dowlatrao had to be stopped. Since the departure of Dowlatrao Sindia from the Deccan the work remained in the same neglected condition for several years. About 1830 Maharaja Jankoji Sindia, the great-grandson of Mahadji, resumed the work of the monument, but he too died in 1842 leaving it unfinished. Since that time the tomb enjoyed a yearly allowance of Rs. 3,500 which was spent in performing a daily worship customary in such tombs and distributing food and charity to the poor on the anniversary day of the great Maratha hero in February every year.

Recently the most enlightened and energetic ruler of Gwalior, H. H. the Maharaja Madhavrao Sindia, while on a visit to Poona, noticed the miserable condition of the tomb of his illustrious ancestor, and considering it his first duty to perpetuate the memory of that great statesman, sanctioned a munificent grant for the purpose. The present handsome Chhatri, a conical edifice of immense proportions, which attracts the attention of every visitor to Wanavdi, is the noble work of the high-minded Maratha Prince of Gwalior whose reverence and regard for the memory of his ancestor are exemplary. The main building is in the centre of a court-yard open from all sides. The style of architecture is rather interesting. It consists of tiers of miniature Chhatris surrounding the principal one. The entrance to the court-yard is by way a gate-house of novel construction, consisting of pavilions supported on the figure-heads of elephants gaily painted. In the interior of the main temple, there is a dimly lighted cell, and in a recess is the sacred statue of Maharaja Mahadji Sindia in whose honour this monument has been erected.

It may be mentioned here that the painting seen by Sir James Mackintosh and mentioned as the work of Zoffany is not now visible here, but has been taken to Gwalior by the present Maharaja and carefully preserved as a historic relic. A photograph of this picture has been reproduced in that interesting book on John Zoffany by Lady Victoria Manners who remarks :— "One notable portrait should be mentioned here.

It was whilst he was at Agra that Zoffany most probably painted the portrait of Mahadji Scindia (Madhavrao Scindia, the Maratha Chief 1759-1795) who conquered Delhi in 1789 and which is referred to by Sir James Mackintosh in the journal of his visit to Poona in 1805." But on inquiry I learn that this painting is not the original work of Zoffany, but of the famous artist James Wales, who was introduced to the Peshwa by Sir Charles Malet, British Resident at Poona. At this time Mahadji Sindia was there, and the original letters of those days prove beyond doubt that the Peshwa, Nana Phadnavis, Mahadji Sindia and other Maratha nobles patronized the artist. In a letter of 1794 it is mentioned that "the artist engaged by Mahadji Sindia visited the Peshwa and showed the sketch of Mahadji Sindia to him; the late Sindia's clerk, Bhiwajipant, suggested to the Peshwa that since the death of Patil Bawa Mahadji Sindia) the artist was in great affliction. Then the Peshwa remarked that the Patil Bawa was a true appreciator of real merits and nobody would take his place again." This fully supports the view that the portrait was the work of Wales or his assistants who were engaged by the great Sindia for portraying himself at Poona. The present writer fortunately possesses an original sketch of this celebrated personage by Wales which is reproduced here. James Wales and his assistant Robert Mahon had drawn several portraits of the notable chieftains in Poona and the painting in question may be one of their works.

The name of Mahadji Sindia is famous in Maratha history. His father Ranoji, originally a Patil or headman of Kanherkhed, a village in the Satara district, rose to distinction in the Peshwa's army. By his wonderful ability and military instincts he gained the favour of his master Bajirao I, who bestowed on him a Jahagir or fief in Malwa. His elder son, Dattaji, and grandsons Jayappa and Jankoji, were gallant soldiers, and played a conspicuous part in the wars against the Rajputs and the Moguls in Northern India and were slain on the battle-field. Mahadji, the younger son of Ranoji, was present in the disastrous battle of Panipat and narrowly escaped death. His character and his achievements are so remarkable and wonderful that he is considered to be the greatest Maratha statesman and warrior next to Shivaji, who attained a greater, if not more consolidated power, than any Indian prince since the death of Aurangzeb. Major Tone, Commander of the Regiment of Infantry in the service of the Peshwa, who had personally known

SIR MOUNTSTUART ELPHINSTONE, LAST RESIDENT OF THE PESHWA'S COURT (1810-1818).

Mahadji Sindia, writes:—"Mahadji was the only Chief of the Empire who effectually raised a body of foot upon the European system. He was a man of the most enlarged mind and his ambition was equal to his abilities. At the period of his returning to the Deccan in 1791, he was actually Vazir to the Emperor, and came to Poona with the express intention of obtaining the situation of Dewan to the Peshwa; and had he succeeded he would have possessed a larger authority than ever was enjoyed by any of the Emperors in the fullest zenith of their power. A man actuated by views of this extensive kind, could only think upon the great scale, and his successes have been answerable to the magnitude of the undertaking. He established founderies at Agra for the casting of cannon, made all his own arms, gave encouragement to European officers of merit to enter his service, and above all, was fortunate enough to meet with De Boigne, his General of Infantry: a man of first rate talents as an officer, and of consummate knowledge as a politician whose splendid abilities displayed upon a noble theatre, increased the dominions of Sindia to double their original extent and created for himself a princely fortune by a series of successful and honourable labours." Sindia's authority and prestige were raised to the highest degree by his victory over Gulam Kadir and the restoration of the Emperor to the throne at Delhi in 1788. In fact he held the Mogul principality of Delhi and the titular Emperor under his sway.

Having thus established his supremacy in Hindustan, Mahadji came to Poona in 1792 to present the Peshwa with the deeds and robes of the hereditary office of the Vakil-i-Mutalik, or chief minister, and to receive at the hands of his master, the deputy ministership of the same office for himself. He held a great Durbar in his camp near the Sangam and performed the ceremony with greatest pomp. Grant Duff gives a most graphic description of the ceremony :—

" A grand suite of tents was pitched at a distance from his own camp. The Peishwa proceeded towards them with the most pompous form. At the further end of these splendid apartments, a throne, meant to represent that of the Emperor of the Moghuls, was erected, on which was displayed the imperial firmans, the khillut, or dresses of investiture, and all the principal insignia. The Peishwa on approaching the throne made his obeisance thrice, placed 101 gold mohurs upon it as a nuzur or offering, and took his seat on its left. Scindia's Persian secretary then read the imperial firmans and amongst others the edict which prevented the slaughter of bullocks and cows. The Peishwa then received the khillut, consisting of nine articles of dress, five superb ornaments of jewels and feathers, a sword and shield, a pencase, a seal and inkstand, and two royal morchuls, or fans of peacocks' tails, accompanied by a nalkee, a palkee ; a horse and an elephant ; besides six elephants bearing the imperial standard, two crescents, two stars, and the Orders of the Fish and of the Sun. The Peishwa retired to an adjoining tent and returned clothed in the imperial khillut, when he resumed his seat ; and Scindia, followed by Nana Furnuwees and such of the Peishwa's officers as were present, offered nuzurs of congratulation. When the Peishwa arose to return to his palace he was followed by Scindia and Hurry Punt carrying the morchuls and fanning him. He entered Poona seated in the nalkee ; the concourse of people assembled to witness the procession was exceedingly great ; the pomp and grandeur displayed was beyond anything that the inhabitants of Poona had ever seen, whilst the clang of thousands of musical instruments, the shouts of the populace, volleys of musketry, and salvos of cannon, seemed to give all the effect that the projector of this state ceremony could possibly desire."

The real object of Mahadji Sindia in coming to Poona and bringing the imperial titles and insignia to the Peshwa was to gain his confidence and establish his influence in the Poona Durbar. Nana Phadnavis was shrewd enough to know the object of Sindia, and tried to guard against his influence on the young Peshwa ; but the frank and amiable nature and polite manners of the Maratha statesman, and his most agreeable and attractive ways of winning the young mind such as hunting, hawking and other sporting excursions naturally had their effect, and in a short time Sindia became a powerful person in the Poona Durbar. He built for himself a new mansion at Wanavdi, the ruins of which are still visible. He had several ambitious schemes in his mind and would have carried them out, had he lived for a few years more. But unfortunately his life was cut short by the cruel hand of death, and he died in his residence at Wanavdi on the 12th February 1794. Sindia's death was a great loss to the Maratha Empire. His body was cremated at the bank of a stream not far away from his mansion, where now stands the fine monument erected by his worthy descendant, known as 'Sindia's Chhatri.'

V.

POONA AND ITS RULERS.

Poona is a very old province, which is situated on the borderland of Mawal and Desh, and seems to have been the chief route for communication and trade since long ages. It formed the junction of routes from the seaport of Kalyan to the country inside and from the Deccan in the south to the Malwa in the north. The many inscriptions and caves in the vicinity of Poona show that it was an important province in those days. The earliest mention of Poona is found in a copper plate recently discovered at Talegaon. This plate was engraved by the King Krishnaraj of the Rashtrakuta dynasty, in authentication of a gift given in Shaka 690, *i.e.*, 768 A.D. on the occasion of a Solar eclipse on the last day of Vaishakh of the Shaka year 690, *i.e.*, on the 23rd March 768. The gift given on this occasion was the village of Kumarigram (Koregaon) which is described to have been bounded by the village of Khamgaon on the east; Khadir Hills on the south; Alandi and Theur on the west, and the river Mula on the north, and is specifically mentioned as lying in the district of 'Punnak.' From some five specimens of granite collected by Lord Valentia in the vicinity of Poona, the writer in the Poona Gazetteer suggests the name 'Poona' to be identical with 'Punnat' mentioned by Ptolemy in 150 A.D. for being well-known for agate stones and this surmise is confirmed by a map drawn in about 1673 by the early English traveller Fryer in which Poona is spelt as 'Panatu.' However it may be, we have the name Poona clearly mentioned for the first time in the year 768, when, as the copper plate shows, that province was under the Hindu Kings of the Rashtrakuta dynasty. Before the Rashtrakutas, the province was under the rule of the Andhras as is shown by the discovery of some silver coins at Junnar near Poona. After this period we find no mention of this province anywhere in the history till the year 1340, when Mahommad Taghlak of Delhi, after having subjugated the Hindu Yadav Kings of Devgiri, sent a large force against the fort of Kondana (the present Sinhagad) which is 13 miles to the south of Poona. It seems that Kondana was then an important fort. Even before 1340 Poona seems to have been taken once by the troops of Allauddin Khilji, Emperor of Delhi. Since 1340 Poona was under the Mahomedan sway till the year 1595 when along with three other villages and forts it was bestowed by the king Bahadur Nizam of Ahmednagar as a Jahagir upon Maloji Bhonsle, the grandfather of Shivaji, the illustrious founder of the Maratha Empire. After the kingdom of Ahmednagar was absorbed into the Bijapur kingdom, Maloji's son Shahaji was confirmed in his old grant by the Bijapur king, and since then excepting the short period during which Shahistekhan, a commander of Aurangzeb, had occupied it, Poona remained in the hands of the Marathas till the year 1818 when the Maratha Empire crumbled to pieces.

Poona was at first only a small collection of a few huts. It derived its significance from the confluence of two rivers the Mula and the Mutha— such confluences of rivers being always looked upon as sacred by the Hindus. Near the confluence was a temple named 'Punyeshwar' from which perhaps the word Poona was derived. This temple was afterwards pulled down by the Mahomedans and a *darga* or shrine was erected in its place, now known as the 'Shaikh Salla.' The rise of Poona may be dated from the year 1635 when the grant of the village of adjoining territory was confirmed upon Shahaji Bhonsle, who made Poona a place of his residence and built there a palace ' Lal-mahal ' where he kept his wife, Jijabai, and his son, Shivaji. He also appointed a Brahmin deputy, Dadaji Kondadeo, to look after his family and estate. Poona owes much of its prosperity and development to Dadaji, who reduced rents of lands and encouraged cultivation. As Shivaji grew up and raised a rebellion against the Bijapur kingdom, Poona came into greater prominence and became Shivaji's headquarters till the year 1674, when Shivaji shifted it to Raygad, where his coronation took place. Raygad then became the capital of the Maratha kingdom and remained so till the capture of Sambhaji by Aurangzeb in 1689. Rajaram, Shivaji's younger son, ultimately fixed his capital at Satara. Shahu who succeeded Shivaji, the son of Rajaram, also settled at Satara in 1708. In the struggle for independence that ensued between the Moghuls and the Marathas after Shivaji's death, Poona was tossed between the two powers, and though Dhanaji Jadhav captured it from Lodikhan in 1707, the Moghuls and the Marathas both claimed their right over it. In fact, Poona was under a sort of double government till the year 1720, when under the grant from the Emperor of Delhi, Poona became one of Shahu's sixteen Swarajya districts. Shahu's representative at Poona was Balaji Vishwanath who, first styled

Sarsubhedar, subsequently became the Peshwa, the founder of the well-known Peshwa dynasty. 'Peshwa' is a Persian word which signifies the meaning 'the foremost' and was introduced in politics as a title by the Bahmini kings. It is equivalent to Prime Minister or Premier. It was adopted by Shivaji who appointed in 1656 his first minister Shamrajpant as Peshwa. In 1674 when he was crowned at Raigad, he made Moropant Pingle his Peshwa or Chief Minister amongst the Asht-pradhans or cabinet of eight. The office was continued to the Pingle family till 1714 when Raja Shahu, grandson of Shivaji, appointed Balaji Vishwanath Bhat as his Peshwa. The office became hereditary and lasted for six eventful generations. It is not possible to narrate here the historical account of this illustrious family but only to give a short out-line from 1714 to 1818.

Balaji Vishwanath was a Chitpawan or Konkanasth Brahman. Raja Shahu selected him to be his Peshwa on account of his superior energy and talents. "He had," writes Sir Richard Temple, once a Governor of Bombay, "a calm, comprehensive and commanding intellect, an imaginative and aspiring disposition, and an aptitude for ruling rude natures by moral force, a genius for diplomatic combinations, a mastery of finance."

Such an able man was sure to take advantage of the opportunities and benefit his master. His crowning achievement was the grant of Swarajya to Raja Shahu from the Mogul Emperor or the full recognition of the territories which Shivaji possessed at the time of his death and the Sardesmukhi or 10 per cent. revenue over the Deccan. Having earned a great fame as the most successful and able minister, Balaji Vishwanath died at Saswad, a village near Poona, in 1720.

Bajirao, the eldest son of Balaji Vishwanath, was appointed Peshwa by the Raja Shahu. In addition to the manly training from his father he possessed an engaging manner, a winning address and an adventurous spirit which made him fit for responsible position. He extended the Maratha dominion by conquest to the south and to the north, and earned the reputation of a brave and successful military leader rather than of a constructive administrator. His invasions into Malwa, Gujarat, and the Carnatic and his victories over the Nizam, Mahomed Khan Bungash and other powerful rivals, were full of glory for the Marathas and a terror to his enemies. He did not possess the business tact and practical wisdom in financial matters like his father, and the state finances in his time were always in a straitened condition. "He died as he had lived," justly remarks Sir Richard Temple, "in camp under canvas among his men, and he is remembered to this day among Marathas as the fighting Peshwa or the incarnation of Hindu energy." Bajirao first conceived the idea of making Poona his headquarters instead of Saswad. In 1728 he gave sites to his five Sardars for building their mansions and in 1732 built his own palace, the well-known Shanwar Wada. This soon increased the importance of Poona; merchants and traders came and settled there. Yet Poona did not become the real capital of the Maratha Empire till Raja Shahu's death in 1749, when the whole power came to be concentrated in the hands of the Peshwas.

To trace the growth of Poona we must go back to the date of the first Mussulman conquest. When the village was captured by the Mahomedans, they stationed there an Arab Commander by name 'Barrya' who first fortified the town by a mud wall with three gates. The ruins of this wall still remain. The town inside the wall was known as 'Kasba' and was inhabited only by garrisons and Mahomedans. The Hindus, especially the trading population, lived outside the wall. As the town prospered and extended, four new wards or Peths were added, two to the south, one to the east and one to the west.

Southern Peths were called Mohiyabad and Malkapur, which are now known as the Budhwar and Aditwar. The eastern Peth was called Astapura, now known as Mangalwar, and the Western Peth Murchadabad is now called the Shanwar Peth. During the war between the Ahmednagar and Bijapur kingdoms, Poona had its full share of rapine and famine. In 1630 when Shahji was pursued by the Bijapur army, Murar Jagdeo, a commander of the Bijapur king, burnt the town, pulled down its walls, and drove an ass plough through the foundations. As a sign that the place was cursed, he planted an iron rod on the ground. Poona, however, survived this curse and flourished under Dadaji Kondadeo, when Shahji was won over into the Bijapur service after the fall of Ahmednagar and was confirmed in his Jahagir by the King of Bijapur in 1635. To remove the curse laid down by Murar Jagdeo, Dadaji threw away the iron rod and got the land ploughed with a golden plough and made it the residence of Shahji's wife Jijabai and her son Shiwaji Jijabai built a temple to Ganpati which is still in existence and is known as the Kasba Ganpati.

Since Poona became a place of residence of the Peshwas its growth was rapid. In 1739, only seven years after Bajirao came and settled there, Captain Gordon, a British envoy to Satara, visited Poona, who found many signs of prosperity there. In the city the streets were crowded and the houses handsome. There were munition and gun factories where great guns were cast, and the weaving industry was so prosperous that the produce of Poona looms was exported to various parts in India and particularly to Bombay. The rent of land was low and agriculture was in a flourishing condition. Bajirao and his son Balaji had however little time to develop the town being mostly engaged in warfare. Bajirao died in 1740 and was succeeded by his son Balaji *alias* Nanasaheb. For the first four years of his reign there was peace, and the young Peshwa could devote his time in improving the administration of Poona. Shahu died in 1749 and before his death Nanasaheb obtained from him a deed empowering him to manage the whole of the Maratha Empire. This naturally centred .all the power into the hands of the Peshwa and Poona virtually became the capital of the Maratha Empire. A French Missionary Tieffenthalers visiting Poona in 1750 describes it the capital of a Brahman Prince and well peopled. Another Frenchman, Du Perron, a scholar and traveller, who visited Poona seven years later, writes that Poona was the union of four or five villages with a common market and some one-storeyed houses. The market was a broad street which crossed the town from end to end, and contained shops exhibiting merchandise from Asia and Europe. Some runaway Europeans also are described to have lived in the market. The rest of the town was not worthy of note.

It is not contemplated here to enter into the history of the rise and fall of the Peshwas, nor to dwell at length upon their foreign and internal affairs. Suffice it to say that Balaji Bajirao was a man of skilful address and great ability. He organized campaigns and led armies and utilized the talents of young Maratha shilledars like Sindia, Holkar, Pawar and others in achieving the highest success. In his reign the Maratha power reached its zenith. He introduced a better system in every branch of administration and considerably improved the condition of the peasantry. After such a brilliant and successful career came the tragic end. The fatal defeat at Panipat was too much for the Prince, who died broken-hearted at Parvati in 1761.

Madhav Rao I succeeded his father Balaji Bajirao as the fourth Peshwa, at the tender age of seventeen only. He possessed high character and virtues of the purer, nobler, loftier quality. By ability, talents and courage, the young Peshwa quickly retrieved the lost prestige and seems to

have paid considerable attention to the development and internal administration of Poona. He appointed the celebrated Ramshastri as his Chief Justice and the famous Nana Phadnavis as his Secretary. Madhav Rao's career was exceptionally brilliant but unfortunately short. He died in 1772 in his prime of youth at Theur near Poona leaving his younger brother Narayanrao to succeed him. Sir Richard Temple while praising the administration of this wise ruler says:—
"That Madhu Rao, a Hindu prince, should have done so much in so brief a life as his, under such disadvantages and despite such temptations—that before being cut off in the heyday of his career, he should have evinced such capacity as this, not only in affairs susceptible of management by youthful genius, but also in matters ordinarily demanding the experience of riper years—is truly astonishing. Indeed he is for ever to be revered, as the model prince, the '*flos regum*' and as one of the finest characters that the Hindu nationality has ever produced."

Madhav Rao's uncle, Raghunathrao, a brave and ambitious man, with an equally ambitious woman Anandibai as his wife, was responsible for all the intrigues and misery Poona witnessed in after years. Raghunathrao aspired to the Peshwa's Gadi but Madhav Rao was too strong for him.

After a struggle between them Madhav Rao defeated him in 1768 and confined him in the Peshwa's Palace at Poona. Raghunathrao waited for his opportunity till 1772, when young Narayanrao came to the Gadi. A dastardly plot was planned and Narayenrao was brutally murdered in his palace on the 30th August 1773, only a few months after his accession. Raghunathrao then assumed the title of Peshwa, but the ministers being opposed to him formed a council of twelve (Barbhai), refused to acknowledge Raghunathrao as Peshwa, and declared that the administration would be carried on in the name of Narayanrao's widow, Gangabai, who was pregnant at the time. She was removed for safety to Purandhar where she shortly gave birth to a son who was proclaimed Peshwa under the name Sawai Madhav Rao. Raghunathrao continued to be a thorn in the sides of the ministers till his death in 1784 and his intrigues sowed the seed of those dissensions in the Poona government which led to its fall.

Nana Phadnavis who was the chief minister of Sawai Madhav Rao devoted his talents and energy in improving the administration, as well as the city which had undergone so many reverses since the death of Madhav Rao I. A town which was described as prosperous and wealthy in 1757 was according to Captain Renell in 1785, " meanly

NANA PHADNAVIS, CHIEF MINISTER AT POONA (1750-1800).

built, not large and defenceless". But under the administration of Nana Phadnavis the town thrived quickly, and when Captain Moor visited it in 1792 he found the neighbourhood of Poona well watered and adorned by gardens and groves; the city was not large, but fairly built and some of the houses were elegant. There were large markets full of English articles, looking glasses, globes, lamps and other finery. Moor remarks that the Police was particularly well regulated.

The year 1792 was memorable on account of the grand ceremony the city witnessed of investing the young Peshwa with title of Vakil-i-Mutalik, given by the Emperor of Delhi. This title was won for him by the Maratha general, Mahadji Sindia, who brought the Sanad and dress of honour with him from Delhi and invested the Peshwa amidst the greatest pomp and ceremony Poona had ever seen. Mahadji died after a short illness in 1794 at Wanavdi near Poona. In October 1795 the young Peshwa also died of a fall from the terrace of his palace upon a fountain jet below.

With the death of Sawai Madhav Rao, good days of the Maratha Empire were over. In later years Poona was a hot-bed of intrigues, plots, plunder and immorality. The glory and splendour of the Peshwas reached their zenith in the time of Sawai Madhav Rao and soon after his death the decline began; the people and military showed little respect to authority. In 1797 there was a desperate affray in the streets of Poona between a body of Arab soldiers and a party of Marathas which resulted in the death of more than 100 persons and the plunder of many houses and shops. The spot on which this riot took place is still known as Khunya Murlidhar.

Sawai Madhav Rao was succeeded by Bajirao, the son of Raghunathrao, much against the wish of the ministers. Bajirao was licentious and cowardly having none of the good qualities which had made his ancestors able rulers. As soon as he came to the Gadi, he won over Dowlatrao Sindia who was already jealous of Nana's influence and power, and with his help got Nana arrested and imprisoned in the Ahmednagar fort. All the friends and partisans of the minister together with the people who were against Raghunathrao were also similarly arrested and imprisoned and their houses plundered. This caused great consternation and indignation throughout the city, but the flood-gates of anarchy and oppression were now let loose and the Empire that took 150 years to rise crumbled down within less than twenty years. In 1798 another and still greater calamity awaited the city and its inhabitants. Bajirao owed a large amount of money to Dowlatrao Sindia for the help he had received from him but was unable to return it. He therefore suggested to Sindia that the amount might be levied from the inhabitants. The hint was enough and Sarjerao Ghatge, a most cruel and unscrupulous man, who was the father-in-law of Sindia plundered the town so cruelly and ferociously that his name is still remembered with horror. Meanwhile Nana Phadnavis was released from prison and put at the head of the administration, but he did not live long and died in the year 1800. It is admitted by historians that his death sealed the fate of the Peshwa's kingdom. Col. Palmer, the British Resident, wrote that "with him has departed all the wisdom and moderation of the Maratha Government."

Bajirao now openly showed his vindictive policy and avenged himself on all men who had opposed him and his father. Among them was Madhav Rao Raste, whom Bajirao invited to the Palace and arrested there. This produced great consternation in the city which soon became a scene of plunder and lawlessness. Vithojirao, the brother of Yeswantrao Holkar, who had helped Bajirao against Sindia, was also arrested in an affray, and Bajirao ordered him to be trampled under an elephant's feet.

With all this disorder and anarchy Poona was still prosperous as evinced by Colonel Welsh and Captain Robertson in 1801. The town was at this time about three miles in length and had 1,40,000 houses and 6,00,000 population. Some of the streets were extremely narrow, and full of shops containing merchandise from India, Europe and China. Some houses were three or four storeyed high and looked pretty from the opposite side of the river which presented a very beautiful view of the Ghats on its bank, intermingled with trees. The fruit markets in the town were rich with various fruits and vegetables. Captain Robertson describes Poona as a rich, gay and busy city, as governors and other big people made money outside and came to Poona to spend it on marriages, feasts and other enjoyments. " Vast wealth flowed into Poona from other causes, the intrigues of foreign powers and the deference shown to the Peshwa by the Maratha leaders. The city was bright with bands of armed men, handsome horses, rich palanquins and gorgeous elephants ; messengers ran from place to place, all was gay with sport, dances and merry-making."

In 1802 Poona had again the misfortune to be plundered by Yeshvantrao Holkar who came down to take revenge for his brother's disgraceful death. He defeated the Peshwa's army near

Poona, whereupon Bajirao immediately fled to Sinhagad. Holkar took possession of the city and at first showed great moderation. He established order in the town and made several attempts to induce Bajirao to return to Poona. But Bajirao fled to the Konkan and asked the English for their help in restoring him to the Peshwa's Gadi. This news made Holkar furious and he levied a contribution from the inhabitants of the town, which was followed by a plunder as cruel and severe as that by Ghatge. Several big houses were pulled down in the search for treasures and the Peshwa's own palace, Shanwar Wada, did not escape from his hands. In order to restore peace at Poona the English Government agreed to place Bajirao on the throne, and the well-known treaty of Basseign was signed on the 31st December 1802. By it the Peshwa agreed to keep a subsidiary force of six battalions with guns, and ceded a territory worth Rs. 26,00,000 for their expenses. General Wellesley brought the Peshwa to Poona and installed him on the Gadi in April 1803.

The internal political situation of Poona however continued to grow from bad to worse, and the population and wealth of Poona also began to dwindle. The population mentioned by Col. Welsh in 1801 as 6,00,000 was only about a lac in 1808 when Sir James Mackintosh visited the place. Another English visitor writing in 1816 says about Poona that "in point of strength the city was not worth much consideration but its vast wealth and its Brahmin Government gave it an importance among the Maratha States."

Bajirao's foolishness and treachery hastened the downfall of the Maratha power; and the battle of Kirkee on the 5th of November 1817 closed the last chapter in the Maratha History. The last of the Peshwa's army was signally defeated in this battle and its leaders were either killed or dispersed. After the flight of Bajirao, Poona was in a helpless condition and was an easy prey to pillage and oppression at the hands of lawless and desperate soldiers. The city was at last surrendered on the 17th November 1817 and on that eventful day the British flag was hoisted on the Peshwa's palace and the Maratha Empire came to an end. Bajirao and his troops were pursued and defeated by the British Army in Central India. Being thus overpowered, the last Peshwa surrendered on the 3rd June 1818 to Sir John Malcolm and agreed to retire to Bithur near Cawnpur on a pension of 8 lacs a year. He died there on the 28th January 1851 and thus ended the Peshwa dynasty.

VI.

THE POONA POLICE.

Ghashiram Kotwal.

Poona was a small village before it became the residence of Baji Rao I in 1730 and there was no such separate and well organised Police Department in the old days. According to Elphinstone every village made its own arrangements for the safety of its people and property, and the Patil or the headman was responsible for the Police of his village. In maintaining peace and order he was aided by the Kulkarni and the Chougula of the village and when necessary by all the inhabitants. But the responsible assistant of the Patil in this matter was the village watchman called Mhar or Taral. His duties were to keep watch at night, to find out all arrivals and departures, to observe all strangers and report all suspicious persons to the Patil. The watchman was likewise bound to know the character of each man in the village, and in the event of a theft committed within the village bounds, it was his business to detect it. For this service he received his allowance in kind and cash.

The Patil exercised the same authority as a Police officer as he did as a revenue one. The mamlatdar in his turn held both the duties, Police and Revenue, and was subordinate to the Sar-subhedar who kept the same superintendence over the mamlatdar. These officers had considerable establishments to maintain peace in the district. They had *Shibandis* or irregular infantry and the small parties of horse which were kept in every district to keep peace and order. It was their chief duty to oppose violence and to support the village Police. Such were the arrangements in the village and the district of Poona upto the time of Baji Rao I. Poona acquired its later importance only after Baji Rao made it his chief place of residence and built the Shanwar Wada in 1730. Thenceforth it gradually grew into a town but did not achieve its true importance till the death of Raja Shahu in 1749, when the virtual powers of the Maratha Empire came to be transferred to the Peshwas. Baji Rao and his son Balaji did not stay long in Poona as they were engaged during most of their time in *Mulukhgiri* or conquering territories and extending the Maratha kingdom. It was however in the reign of Balaji that some attention was paid to improving and organizing the home administration. But he too being engrossed in foreign politics and invasions did not find much leisure to create a regular Police department in Poona. At the end of his career came the heavy shock of the defeat of the Marathas at Panipat and he died a broken-hearted man in 1761, leaving all his schemes and plans for execution to his able son Madhav Rao I, the fourth Peshwa, who greatly improved the Police in Poona.

By this time Poona had become the chief capital of the Marathas and consequently the true centre of all Maratha activities. It had naturally risen in population and importance. The Peshwa Madhav Rao the Great, saw the necessity of organizing a separate Police establishment for the City and created for the first time a regular office of Kotwal or the Head of Police, and appointed Balaji Narayan Ketkar, the first Kotwal in 1764. He was independent of the Head Police Superintendent and communicated direct with the Ministers of the Peshwa. He had a large establishment consisting of some horse and a considerable body of *shibundis*. Chowkis were placed in and about the city, parties of horse patrolled outside, and there were frequent round of *shibundis* inside the town during the night. A gun was fired at 11 o'clock, after which no person could stir out of his house unattended by a particular peon, until 4 o'clock in the morning, when, on another signal of gun, the restriction ceased.

There were Ramoshis employed who became answerable for all thefts, and who were bound to restore the property or to pay its value. It needs no mention that the duties of this office were not quite similar to those of the Superintendent of Police of the present day. The Kotwal had not only to look to the safety of the town and its people, but had to do many other things. He had power to settle trifling disputes and to redress petty grievances. He superintended bazars, inspected weights and measures, and also held control over musicians, concubines, barbers and such kind of people. Besides these he had to perform miscellaneous duties such as the sanitation of the city, the repairs and construction of public roads, drainage and buildings, attendance on distinguished visitors, distribution of public charity, and registration of documents. He had also to investigate offences, political and otherwise, and had to detect and discover political conspiracies. Thus the C. I. D., Magistracy, Municipality, P. W. D., Registration, were all centred in the one office of Kotwal who was so to say the Mayor of the city. He exercised his jurisdiction only within the limits of the city, and even there he had no power over the military and guards at the Palace of the Peshwa, who were subordinate to the officers from the Army. He had also the power to try minor offences such as thefts, adultery, drinking, gambling, etc., and the fines recovered were credited to the department, to which was also added property forfeited to Government by way of punishment, tax on widow remarriages among lower castes, and fees on registration of deeds, and stamping on weights and measures, and cloth. The income derived from all these sources ranged from rupees thirty to fifty thousand a year. In 1764 the establishment of the Kotwal consisted of five clerks and 18 sepoys, its cost being about Rs. 1,449. In 1768 the office of the Kotwal was given to Janardan Hari when the expenditure on the department was also considerably increased, probably owing to the increase in the population. The instructions issued to Janardan Hari by the Peshwa Madhavrao I were as follows :—

1. Minor disputes in the Peiths and the Kasba should be disposed of by the Kamavisdars of several Peiths, and disputes of importance should be disposed of by the Kotwal.

2. The Kotwal should fix the prices of goods with his own discretion and a list of bazar rates so fixed should be daily submitted to Government.

3. The Kotwal should supply labourers as required by Government from among the artizans and the members of the several castes in the city.

4. Sales and purchases of land sites should be made with the permission of the Kotwal who should prepare necessary documents and receive the fees due to Government.

5. The Kotwal should take the census, and keep a record of all persons coming into and leaving the city. Kamavisdars of the Peiths should supply him with information.

6. The Office of the Kotwal should be held in the place assigned for it in Budhwar Peith.

7. All disputes relating to lanes, roads and houses should be disposed of by the Kotwal.

8. Professional gamblers should not gamble without a written permission of the Kotwal who should levy on them the usual fees. Others should not be allowed to gamble.

9. The Kotwal should receive annually the following sums for himself and his staff as their emoluments :—

Rs.

300 Janardan Hari, Daroga or Kotwal.

200 Bhikaji Narayan Kolhatkar, Phadnis.

150 Naro Shankar Sathe, Daftardar.

500 Four Karkuns, each Rs. 125.

2,114 Policemen—

1,760 Constables each Rs. 40.

260 Recruits.

2,114

110 Two torch-bearers.

100 Orderlies.

144 Vatandars.

3,618

10. The Kotwal should issue orders for any proclamation being made by beat of drum.

11. Should the Kotwal consider any old registration, or any new one to be adopted; he should submit proposals to Government and act in accordance with orders issued by them.

It is worth-noting that the famous Kotwal Chavdi or the office of Kotwal in the Budhwar

Peith came into existence in 1768 and the expenditure on the Police was Rs. 3,264. In the years 1775 and 1776 Anandrao Kashi and Dhondo Babaji were the Kotwals. By this time the establishment of the Kotwal was further enlarged. He was now given six officers under him, one Amin with an annual salary of Rs. 400, Diwan with a salary of Rs. 325, Phadnis with a salary of Rs. 200, and a Daftardar and Potnis with a salary of Rs. 150 and 125 respectively. Besides these higher officers, there were several clerks among whom was one Police Prosecutor, who was paid Rs. 125 a year. The constables and watchmen numbered 78 and the total of their annual salaries amounted to Rs. 5,295.

Since the establishment of the office of Kotwal in 1764, its necessity and importance gradually increased along with the growth of population and wealth in Poona. It appears that clever and intelligent men were selected for this responsible post, and systematic attempts were made to improve the Police in Poona. With all its abuses and drawbacks it has been admitted that the Police system in the Peshwas' time proved successful in maintaining peace and order and preventing crime in the country. It may however be noted that there were a few instances of abuse of power and corruption which were duly punished by the Government when brought to light. There was an extraordinary case of a Kotwal which in the history of the Poona Police deserves special mention for its notoriety.

The name of Ghashiram Kotwal is very famous in history. He was a Kanoja Brahmin, son of Shamaldas or Savaldas. He came from Aurangabad among the many who flocked to Poona from all parts of India to make their fortunes either by service or trade. Possessed of amiable manners, a quick intelligence and an attractive appearance, he easily got an introduction to the Poona Durbar, and secured the favour of Nana Phadnavis. It was then rumoured in Poona that he had a beautiful daughter named Lalitagouri who was the cause of his fortune. Whatever may be the true reason, Ghashiram soon rose to power, and became the Kotwal or head of the Poona Police in 1782. He was no doubt an able and efficient officer and took great pains to improve and enlarge the Police department. From old records we find that the office of Kotwal was taken from Anandrao Kashi and given to Ghashiram Savaldas in 1777, but he was confirmed in the office in 1782. His salary was fixed at Rs. 621 a year including an allowance of Rs. 66 for an attendant to hold

Aftagiri (umbrella) and Rs. 55 for *Divatya* or torch bearer. The following instructions were issued to him when he was appointed Kotwal of Poona :—

1. Clerks and peons employed at the Kotwal's office should not be removed without the consent of Sar-Amin who was appointed by Government.

2. Two new Police posts should be established in Narayan Peith and Shanwar Peith, as owing to want of sufficient Police posts offences in those parts were not detected.

3. The duties of the office should be carried on honestly and in conformity with the established practice.

4. Roads should be kept in good order. New verandahs and sheds, if constructed without permission after the Great Fire in the city should be pulled down.

5. Information should be regularly collected in each Peith regarding conspirators coming into the city and Government should be kept informed about their movements.

6. Proper arrangements should be made to keep watch at night, and thefts should

be detected carefully and offenders sent to Government for trial.

7. 78 peons at a cost of Rs. 310 per year (11 months) were attached to the office and expenses to be incurred as sanctioned by Government.

8. Married women should not be given permission to become prostitutes.

Ghashiram had three officers under him, each for the three different departments entrusted to the care of the Kotwal. The Mujumdar wrote out the writs and deeds, another officer kept the registers and the third was the head revenue officer. The salary of these three officers amounted to Rs. 640 per year. In Ghashiram's time there were six Police stations in the City known as *Chabutras* :—

1. The Kotwal Chavdi.
2. The Somwar Police station.
3. Vetal ,, ,,
4. Aditwar ,, ,,
5. Narayan Peith ,, ,,
6. Shanwar ,, ,,

The income from all these Police stations was about 25,000 rupees per year. With the growth of the population in the city the limited number of Police guards was found to be insufficient, and in 1789, 25 more Police guards were created at a cost of Rs. 3,500. It was estimated that Ghashiram had a charge over a force of about 115 Police constables which number was increased in subsequent years as necessity arose.

It is interesting to note the figures of receipts in 1790-91. The credits during the year were as follows :—

Rs. 315 Nazar—Fines or fees on succession to property.
,, 154 Kamavis.
,, 4,663 Tax on sale of houses.
,, 205 Tax on widow remarriage in lower castes.
,, 61 Fees from musicians.
,, 15,985 Fines.
,, 3,042 Intestate property.
,, 293 Fine on gambling.
,, 2,376 Stamping fees of weights and measures and cloth, etc.

The total comes to Rs. 27,610 which was the income of the Poona Police department. The following were the offences for which fines were imposed :—

2 Becoming prostitutes without the permission of Government.

2 Concealing an offence.

3 Possessing intestate property without informing Government.

2 Disobeying Government orders knowingly.

2 Killing goats without permission.

1 Interring an unclaimed body without Kotwal's permission.

1 False complaint for adultery.

1 Passing counterfeit coin.

8 Drinking (the number of accused persons was 40 only).

2 Concealing one's caste.

2 Dining with caste people though excommunicated.

2 Dining at the hands of a person of a lower caste.

6 Following the profession of a pimp.

5 Abortion.

2 Purchasing girls for prostitution without permission.

3 Indescent assaults on women.

3 Criminal actions on relatives of persons who committed suicide.

1 Mischief.

4 Hurt.

7 Kidnaping women, children and slaves.

20 Theft.

145 Adultery.

2 Remarrying during the life-time of a husband.

2 Living with one's own wife after divorcing her.

2 Disputes regarding commercial transactions.

1 Engaging in the service of Kolis.

The list makes up a total of 234 offences which show the morality of Poona in 1791. From a perusal of the list it can be easily noticed that the offences for sexual immorality were largest which will partially account for the unpopularity of the Kotwal Ghashiram. The corruption and immorality that prevailed in Poona at this period must have allowed full scope for the evil propensities of an adventurer of the type of Ghashiram, who had become very oppressive and high-handed; on account of the support and favour of Nana Phadnavis; and his own misdeeds brought about his end in a most pitiable and cruel way. Captain Moor on the authority of Sir Charles Malet narrates the incident in the following terms :—

"In the year 1791, a period when political parties had caused much animosity in the court and city of Poona, a Brahman, named Gahunsa-Rama, commonly pronounced Gaunsaram, a native of Aurungabad, of the tribe of Gour, warmly patronized by Nana Furnavese, the minister, held the office of Kutwal, and executed it with great ability, activity, and zeal. Toward the end of the month of August of that year, a large party of convivial Brahmans had separated rather late; and thirty-four of them remaining in the streets beyond the regular time after the firing of Bamboora gun, were taken up by the police, and put in the place allotted for such defaulters; and in the morning twenty-one of them were found dead, and the rest scarcely alive. It did not appear that the Kutwal knew even of their imprisonment until the morning when the catastrophe was unhappily discovered; his officers had performed their usual duty in their usual way; still the clamour against Gaunsaram was excessive, and at length rose to such a pitch, that the unfortunate Kutwal is said to have sought refuge in the Peshwa's palace. But even here, in a Brahmanical and royal sanctuary, he was not safe; and the Peshwa, yielding to his fears, gave up the unhappy man into the hands of the frantic mob, headed by a number of Telingas: of which tribe were the unfortunate sufferers. In his prosperity, the respectable Gaunsaram had built a handsome temple and dug a fine tank, close to the city, to which they are highly useful and ornamental ; and hither was the victim dragged, with every species of indignity : he was bound, and the cord was held by a man of the tribe of Bungi (the basest of the Hindus, being employed in moving carrion, night-soil, etc.), and thus amid the revilings of infuriate devils, he was dragged, with every species of ignominy, and by the hands of Brahmans, of the Telinga sect. was stoned to death, hard by his own munificient donation. This sad event occurred on the 31st August 1791, and was seen in part by my deceased and lamented friend Dr. Findlay, Surgeon to out legation at Poona ; who also saw the mangled corpse. I was not there at the time, but have often passed the spot so suited to melancholy, although, perhaps, not unprofitable, sensations. Sir Charles Malet, and Mr. Uhthoff, were at Poona and were much affected by so deplorable an event."

Ghashiram met his end in such a cruel and detestable manner, but it may be said to his credit that with all his defects he well regulated the Poona

Police and established a new Peith known as Nawapura to the east of Bhawani Peith and built a tank and a garden on the road to Hadapsar.

After the death of Ghashiram, Anandrao Kashi was again appointed Kotwal and the following new additional rules were issued in 1794 for the guidance of the Kotwal which were in force till Bajirao II came to the throne in 1796 :—

1. Orders regarding the infliction of fines should not be passed by the Kotwal except at the Chavdi and with the cognizance of the Darakdars and the amount of fines recovered should be duly credited in the accounts.

2. Intestate or stolen property coming into the hands of the Kotwal shall not be taken by him to his house but brought to the Chavdi and sold with the cognizance of the Darakdars the proceeds to be credited in the account.

3. Kunbi and other women brought to the Chavdi on charges of adultery shall be tried at the Chavdi and shall not be taken by him to his house for trial and kept there as done at present.

4. Kunbi women convicted of adultery should be fined and made over to their husbands. They should not be sold as slaves.

In the reign of the last Peshwa the worst disorder prevailed throughout the country and established laws and regulations were neglected. He introduced the pernicious system of letting the office of Kotwal by auction which brought him large sums. The first bidder to this post was Vithoji Naik Gaikwad who was appointed Kotwal and Kamavisdar of several Peiths in 1800, on payment of Rs. 1,12,000 to Government, on account of the expected revenue of the Kotwali and other miscellaneous receipts. In 1810-1811 there was a police force of 1,628 men in Poona, of which 558 were placed at various Police stations to keep order in the city, 167 for night patrol and the rest were utilised in the royal household and other miscellaneous duties. In 1800-01 there were 18 Peiths or wards in Poona and the total revenue realised from them was Rs. 34,547. "In Bajirao's time," writes Sir Mount-Stuart Elphinstone, "9,000 rupees a month was allowed to the officer who had charge of the police at Poona: from this he had to maintain a very large establishment of peons, some horse patrols, and a considerable number of Ramoshis ; besides being answerable for the amount of property plundered, whenever the Peishwa thought proper to call on him. Still his appointment was reckoned lucrative, as the pay of his establishment was very low, and both he and they derived much profit from unavowed exactions. The police, however, was good; on the whole, murders or robberies, attended with violence and alarm, were very rare; and I have never heard any complaints of the insecurity of property."

VII.

FESTIVALS, SPORTS, AND AMUSEMENTS.

AMONGST the public festivals at Poona the Dasara, the Ganpati Festival, and the Holi were celebrated with great rejoicings and the expenditure incurred by the Peshwa's Durbar in this connecion was also on a grand scale. On these occasions all sorts of sports and amusements were included in the programme and a number of people, especially athletes, dancers, actors, musicians and several other performers were collected in Poona.

The Ganpati Festival was annually held in the Peshwa's Palace from the 1st bright day of Bhadrapad to the 10th. On this occasion the Ganpati Rang-Mahal was gaily decorated and all the functions were held there. Beautiful crystal chandeliers and crystal globes as well as mirrors and paintings multiplied the beauties of the scene and shed a brilliant light over the assemblage. There in the centre the Peshwa's musnud with gold brocade work was seen shining. On both the sides the principal Maratha nobles, sardars, shiledars and other darbaris, all arrayed in brilliant costumes and jewels, were seated according to their ranks, and amidst the cries of the chopdars and bhaldars the Peshwa Sawai Madhav Rao entered the Darbar Hall and with a dignifying bearing took his seat on the throne. The whole Durbar presented a picture of varied character and colouring. The singing of musicians, the nach or dancing, the *kathas* or religious sermons and all other performances that were arranged in the programme were duly carried out to the enjoyment of all.

The details of the expenses incurred on account of Ganpati festival in 1795 shows that the number of Gosavi Haridas or religious preachers who performed the *katha* in the Palace was 181, and that the amount paid as rewards to them was Rs. 2,155 exclusive of dresses. The singers were 39 who got Rs. 329. There were 43 sets of dancing girls who received Rs. 1,026 as presents. Other Gurav musicians who played on *Pakhwaj* numbered 43, who were given Rs. 121, and the *Wajantri* who brought 25 sets were rewarded with Rs. 240. On this occasion all household servants of the Palace took part in the festival and contributed much to its success. They also received presents from the Peshwa with sweetmeats. In this festival a number of Brahmins were fed in the Palace and sweetmeats were distributed to the poor. On the last day, the image of Ganpati which was made of painted clay, expressly for the annual celebration, was taken in a flower-decked palanquin to the river and immersed with certain ceremonies by the Peshwa who accompanied the procession.

Vijaya-Dashami, generally known as Dasara. was one of the principal festivals in Poona in the Peshwas' times. The Dasara, according to the common acceptance of the word, lasts ten days but this term correctly applies to the tenth or last day. The first nine days termed Navaratra belong to the distinct festival in honour of Durga or Bhawani. This deity being the favourite object of devotion of the Bhonsle family the Dasara was celebrated as a state function in Satara till the death of Raja Shahu, after which Balaji Bajirao commenced to hold its annual gathering at Poona with equal grandeur and pomp.

It is not possible in a short space to describe the various religious rites performed by the Hindus on this occasion. Really speaking it is an annual commemoration of Rama's victory over Rawan, King of Lanka or modern Ceylon, and his numerous *rakshasas* or demons. The great feature of the ceremony which assumed a political significance was the procession and the state Durbar which is worthy of note. "On the morning of the tenth day," writes Sir John Malcolm, "the Peshwa, with all his chiefs and soldiers, moves out to the camp in the vicinity of the city, each being ranged under his particular banner, mounted on his best horse. dressed in his finest clothes, and with his arms highly polished. Horses, elephants, and camels are all arranged in their gayest trappings, and every corps spreads its gaudiest flags and banners. The whole population of the capital, either as actors or spectators, join in this grand procession, which moves towards the sacred tree, *Shami*, the object of adoration. After the offerings and prayers, the Peshwa plucks some leaves of the tree, on which all the cannon and musketry commence firing. The Peshwa then plucks from a field purchased for the occasion a stalk of jowary or bajree, on which the whole crowd fire off their arms, or shoot arrows, and rush in an instant, and tear up the whole. Each endeavours to procure his share of the spoil; some succeed in carrying off a handful, whilst others content themselves with a few stalks: all however return home with shouts of joy, and the remainder of the day and night is devoted to festivity and mirth. Many other usages prevail at this festival, which are, I believe, peculiar to the Mahrattas; among others, that of sacrificing sheep and buffaloes, sprinkling the blood on the horses with great ceremony, and distributing the flesh of the former to all ranks, Brahmans excepted. The chiefs often give money to enable their soldiers to buy sheep to perform sacrifices, which from furnishing them with a good dinner, are by many considered as the most essential ceremonies of the Dusrah."

On return from the *Simolanghan* the Peshwa held a great ceremonial Durbar in the Palace, and all the military chiefs and sardars, shilledars and darakdars, paid homage by presenting nazars to the Peshwa, and in return they were presented costly dresses of honour according to their rank and dignity. In the year 1794 the Peshwa presented dresses of honour worth Rs. 2,20,144 and amongst the recipients were the following important personages :—

	Rs.
The Raja of Satara, his family and Sardars	27,383
Pant Pratinidhi, his family and Sardars	1,283
Pant Sachiv, his family and Sardars ..	603
Chintamanrao Patwardhan, his family and Sardars	1,238

	Rs.
Parashram Ramchandra, his family and Sardars	1,089
Tukoji Pawar, his family and Sardars.	789
Khanderao Vithal Vinchurkar, his family and Sardars	2,756
Krishnarao Balwant, his family and Sardars	2,398
Hanmantrao Darekar, his family and Sardars	827
Dowlatrao Ghorpade, his family and Sardars	604
Raghuji Bhonsle, his family and Sardars	6,440
Nizam of Hyderabad, his family and Sardars	5,888
Chintamanrao Hari Phadke, his family and Sardars	1,120
Dowlatrao Sindia, his family and Sardars	11,297
Ali Bahadur	2,015

Besides these the cavalry officers and shilledars received clothes of honour worth Rs. 34,033 and 79,703 respectively.

It was also customary on this occasion that Sir Charles Malet, the British Resident at Poona, was given a dress of honour worth Rs. 600-12-0 and his

Vakil Nurruddin Hussein Khan Rs. 294-8-0. All military and civil officers as well as all the heads of departments and every person of note were entitled to receive dresses of honour, and it is interesting to note that the mistresses of Raghunath Rao Peshwa were also included in the list. This custom was in force till the overthrow of the Peshwa's rule in 1818 and was continued by the British Government for many years. The date was afterwards changed from Dasara to the British Sovereign's Birthday ; and the annual Durbar held under the auspices of the Agent for the Sardars in the Deccan at Poona owes its origin to this old practice. It may be mentioned here that in honour of Dasara there were a number of military sports held at Poona which were, like the military tournaments of the present day, most attractive and popular.

The third annual festival that was mainly intended for relaxation and joy of all classes of people was the Holy festival, which was celebrated by the Peshwa in the Palace with considerable interest and zeal. It was a holiday full of merriment and joy, and was celebrated on the full moon day in the month of Falgun (March-April) and lasted for five days. It was in celebration of spring and always looked for by both old and young with great delight. In the times of the Peshwas the utmost license was permitted to all ranks, and during the holiday, people enjoyed freely, amusing themselves in various ways. During this festival, exhibitions of dancing, singing and musical performances were held in the Peshwa's Palace and they were greatly appreciated by the people. Bhavai Gujrathi and Venkat-narasi were the most famous singers of those days. In those days there were no regular dramatic performances but there were some comic actors who played certain parts before the Durbar and received rewards from the Peshwa. It is on record in the Peshwa's diary in 1785 that Balaling Naik and Laxman Gurav of Supa played the parts of *Dash-avatars* or the ten incarnations, of the God in the Peshwa's Palace, for which they were paid a reward of Rs. 30 each and a dress. The holiday ends on the fifth day which is termed *Ranga-Panchami*. On this day coloured water, generally made of saffron and *Palas* flowers (*Butea pondasa*) was profusely thrown at each other through pots and syringes. This ceremony was generally performed at the Hirabag pleasure-house by the Peshwas, when chiefs and noblemen like Sindia Holkar, and Bhonsle were specially invited. Major Broughton, commander of the Resident's escort at the Court of Sindia, who witnessed the scenes of Ranga-Panchami in a Maratha Durbar gives a graphic description of the occasion. He writes :—

> " Such a scene I never witnessed in my life. Figure to yourself successive groups of dancing girls, bedecked with gold and silver lace ; their tawdry trappings stained with patches of *abeer*, and dripping, like so many Naiads, with orange-coloured water ; now chanting the Holee songs with all the airs of practised libertinism, and now shrinking with affected screams beneath a fresh shower from the Muha Raj's engine ; the discord of drums, trumpets, fiddles, and cymbals sounding as if only to drown the other noises that arose around them ; the triumph of those who successfully threw the *abeer*, and the clamours of others who suffered from their attacks ; the loud shouts of laughter and applause which burst on all sides from the joyous crowd : figure to yourself, if you can, such an assemblage of extraordinary objects ; then paint them all in two glowing tints of pink and yellow, and you will have formed some conception of a scene which absolutely beggars all description."

In the times of Bajirao II, the festival of Holi exceeded the limits of decency and it became a scene of grossest indelicacy and immodesty.

Among the most popular sports of the Marathas, athletic sports were cultivated by the people to a considerable degree, and reached their highest development in the times of the Peshwas. The competitions amongst athletes were very keen, particularly in boxing and wrestling. Victory in the last was the highest achievement of an athlete and was rewarded with handsome presents by the Peshwa. The most popular sport of the day was the *Wajra Mushti* which was a combination of boxing and wrestling, and the athletes who played it were called Jethies. Sir Charles Malet and his staff took keen interest in these sports and attended their exhibitions in the Palace. Major Price writes in his diary the following account of this play :—

> " With regard to the performance of those athletes I should state, that there is usually excavated for the purpose, a circular pit, with perpendicular sides, about 7 feet deep, and perhaps 30 feet in diameter, the bottom well covered with sand. The jetties are naked, with the exception of a pair of very short drawers. Their hands are armed with a kind of cestus, made of horn, shaped into knuckles, and drawn on the fingers. The performance included both boxing and wrestling ; and the performers on this occasion, had evidently

been well and carefully trained. The young Peshwa appeared to be delighted with exhibition, and not the less so when the pugilists repeatedly saluted him as '*Dekhanki-Badshah*'—Emperor of the Dekhan. He was at this period scarcely twenty and a very personable, engaging looking young man."

The famous athletes or Jethies of the times of Sawai Madhav Rao were Govinda Jethi, Mina Jethi and Timma Jethi who were entitled to dresses of honour on the Dasara day worth Rs. 150, 147 and 99½ respectively. Over these sports all Marathas from the Peshwa to a cavalryman were very keen.

The Peshwas were fine riders and excelled in the art of lancing, fencing and swordsmanship, being specially trained in all these manly exercises. Mr. Robert Mabon who was an eye-witness to lance exercises of the Peshwa Sawai Madhav Rao in 1794, gives the following interesting description :—

"I was gratified with a sight of this Prince exercising the long spear, with Purseram Bhow, and other celebrated Mahratta Chiefs. The part which he chose for this purpose, was a large plain, at the bottom of a hill, termed Parbuttee, on account of a small pagoda or temple at the top of it, in which was placed a

SAWAI MADHAVRAO TAKING LANCE EXERCISES.

representation of the Hindoo goddess of that name. A vast number of sepoys and other attendants surrounded the space, which was allotted for the purpose of his exercising : in the centre was placed a small pile of stones. The Peshwa after riding round the course with a long spear, on the end of which was stuck a small ball covered with red cloth, approached the little pile at full gallop : he struck it and it fell ; after which he retreated loudly applauded for his successful effort."

"Purseram Bhow next advanced in the same manner ; he aimed at the pile with his spear, but did not hit it ; several other chiefs made the like attempt, but none were successful. One of them afterwards rode furiously round the course, pursued by the Peshwa, who endeavoured to unhorse him with his spear : he defended himself whilst retreating, but the Prince by his superior skill in the use of the spear, soon accomplished what he pursued him for. I was highly pleased to see such exquisite feats of horsemanship. Their horses were thoroughly trained for the purpose. On a full gallop, at the word of command given, they would make a full stop. The Mahrattas, in general, spare no trouble in training this noble animal for the field."

It may be worth mentioning here that the Peshwas were very fond of elephant fights, and had specially trained their elephants for this purpose. William Price, a member of the Bombay Government, who came to Poona on an embassy in 1759 mentions in his diary :—

> " Sunday 30th, Nana (Balaji Bajirao) sent me an invitation to a tent pitched without the town, where he entertained me with the combats of elephants, which lasted for three hours."

Such animal fights were generally arranged on the occasions of entertaining distinguished guests and for that purpose a number of animals were kept and trained in the Peshwa's menagerie at Poona.

In the park at the foot of Parvati was the menagerie or zoological garden, a fine collection of animals, birds, reptiles and fish. Altogether there were more than a hundred animals. This collection of animals was unique of its kind in the Deccan and there was a regular department opened in Poona by Nana Phadnavis for its up-keep. Major Price who visited Poona in 1791 had seen the Peshwa's menagerie :—

> " During my residence at Poona," writes Major Price, "I do not recollect that any thing

made a more lively impression on my mind, than a visit which, in company with some of our friends from the Sungum, I paid to the Peshwa's menagerie, at the foot of the hill of Pahrbutty. It then contained some of the finest, if not the very finest, specimens of the brute creation that I had ever beheld. There were, in particular, a lion and rhinoceros ; as perfect in their condition and proportions as if they had been at large in their native wilds. The king of animals and lord of the forest, appeared full worthy of his awful dignity. He was in full flesh, perfectly clean ; and presented a forehead of such stately and massive proportions, that taken altogether, as a symbol of majesty, activity and strength, there seemed in all nature nothing comparable. Being uncaged and in an open shed, chained only to a strong upright post driven into the ground, the air had sufficient access all around, so as to prevent the nauseous effluvia, which we experience when these animals are more closely confined. The tranquil indifference with which the majestic creature, seated on his hind legs, and presenting his stupendous chest and forearm, contemplated his strange visitors, in dress and complexion, so different to what he had been accustomed to, could not but impress us with a peculiar sensation of awe. And now, more than ever, I could not be surprised that the celebrated Alep Arslan, should, in the disposition of his hair and beard, have endeavoured to exhibit some resemblance to the features of this most formidable of animals. In this noble creature, at the same time, from its being regularly fed and carefully attended, we had an opportunity of beholding a sample of the species in much higher perfection, than by a transient view in the solitude of the wilderness ; or the exhibitions at Exeter 'Change' in its most flourishing state."

" Next to the lion, and equally as accessible to the fresh air, was, also fastened in the same manner, the finest and most perfect model of a rhinoceros, that I have ever seen, either before or since. For, unlike the shapeless monster that we usually see exhibited, with his body enveloped in loose and flaccid folds of indurated hide, this stupendous animal was filled out to its utmost proportions ; and its huge armour-like exterior being stretched almost to bursting, it was as round as a hogshead ; and at the same time as lively, I was going to say, as any sucking pig. Indeed, when the keeper, by a slight touch with his wand, made him rear up a little on his hind legs, while the alertness surprised me, I could not but compare him to a wine pipe, set a little on one end. At all events, the ponderous agility of the animal was astonishing. Its small, but prominent eye, appeared sparkling, and full of animation ; and the horny mass upon its snout, though it did not yet seem to have attained to its full growth, by its backward turn and hook-like shape, furnished sufficient proof, that when applied by a momentum of such force, its effect must be tremendous ; and renders less surprising the accounts we receive of its power to subdue the otherwise surpassing strength of the elephant. There were several tigers, and other animals in the same range ; but they seemed unworthy of observation, or sunk into insignificance, by the side of the other stupendous creatures."

It may be said to the credit of Sir Charles Malet, the British Resident, who showed considerable interest in this department, presented several animals and birds to this collection which was located at the foot of the Parvati hill, a spot still shown as the Peshwa's *Shikarkhana*.

In this menagerie there was a number of tame deer and antelopes some of which were of a beautiful species and were perfectly familiar. The antelopes had an ear for music and were specially trained in dancing and swinging for the purpose of entertainments. Sir Charles Malet has given an interesting account of an entertainment given by the Peshwa in 1792 :—

"The Peshwa having invited me to a novel spectacle, at his *rumna*, or park, about four miles from Poonah, I proceeded thither about two o'clock in the afternoon, with the gentlemen of my party, where we found a tent pitched for the purpose, and were received at the door by some of the principal nobles. The Peshwa arrived soon after, and when we were all conveniently seated on carpets, agreeably to oriental costume, four black buck antelopes, of noble vein and elegant form, made their appearance at some distance, moving gracefully before a party of cavalry, who forming a semi-circle, gently followed their pace, each horseman holding a long pole, with a red cloth at the end. On approaching the tent, a band of music struck up in loud notes, and three of the antelopes entered in a stately manner. Two swings, commonly used by the Indians, being suspended for the purpose, an antelope ascended on each swing, and couched in the most graceful altitude; the third reclined on the carpet in a similar posture. On the loud music ceasing, a set of dancing girls entered, and danced to softer strains before the antelopes, who chewing the cud, lay in a state of sweet tranquillity and satisfaction. At this time the fourth antelope, who had hitherto appeared more shy than his comrades, came into the tent and laid himself upon the carpet in the same manner. An attendant then put one of the swings in motion, and swung the antelope for some time, without his being at all disturbed. The amusement being continued as long as the Peshwa thought proper, it was closed by the game-keeper placing a garland of flowers over the horns of the principal antelope, on which he rose, and the four animals went off together.

"The Peshwa informed me, that seven months had been employed to bring the antelopes to this degree of familiarity, without the smallest constraint, as they wandered at their pleasure, during the whole time, amongst large herds of deer in the *rumna*; which, although I have mentioned as a park, is not enclosed, nor has it any kind of fence. I was also assured these animals were not impelled by appetite, no grain or food of any kind having been given them: on this I am somewhat of a sceptic. The Peshwa was persuaded they were thus attracted by the power of music; aided, perhaps, by some particular ingenuity of the men who profess the art of familiarizing this beautiful and harmless animal. The Peshwa seemed to be much pleased with the amusement; which in innocence is suited to the tents of the Brahmins, if not to their present character."

Sir Charles Malet had all these animals represented in clay by a clever Brahmin artist who had earned great merit in modelling. A painting of these interesting models, with Sir Charles Malet in the middle, is still in existence and is preserved in the historical collections at Satara.

From this place the Peshwa's hunting reserve was not at a far distance. There was a number of deer in the vicinity of Parvati and the Peshwa Sawai Madhavrao was very fond of their hunt. An amusing incident is recorded in old papers that in 1793, the Peshwa one day chased many a deer and succeeded in capturing some. Mahadji Sindia who happened to be one of the party begged the Peshwa to give him one antelope, but the Peshwa suspecting that Mahadji might

THE PESHWA'S MENAGERIE. (CLAY MODEL PREPARED FOR SIR CHARLES MALET.

kill it, declined the request. The shrewd Maratha quickly understood the reason of the Peshwa's refusal and willingly promised that the animal would be safe with him, whereupon the Peshwa was pleased to grant the favour.

For the pleasure and recreation of human mind gardens and pleasure-houses are also necessary and the Peshwas did not neglect them. In 1791 the following gardens belonging to the Peshwa were famous in Poona :—

1. Hira Bag.
2. Saras Bag.
3. Vasant Bag.
4. Moti Bag.
5. Bag Parvati.
6. Bag Bungalow.
7. Bag Wanavdi.
8. Bag Hingne.
9. Bag Ramana.
10. Bag Wadgaon.
11. Bag Manik.
12. Bag Pashan.
13. Bag Katraj.

Out of these the most noted was the Hira Bag where Balaji Bajirao in 1755 built a pleasure house for himself. Here the Peshwa and his descendants often used to come for recreation and the fêtes in honour of Vasant Panchami were held in this garden. In 1766 a number of feasts were given here in celebration of the marriage of Madhavrao I. Later on in the time of Sawai Madhavrao and Bajirao II, it became the chief place of entertainments to European guests. Lord Valentia who visited Poona in 1803 was entertained here in company of the Resident, Sir Barry Close. He has written a very interesting account of his experience in Hira Bag—particularly about the Hindu dinner of which he partook in oriental fashion. He writes :—

> "At a little after four we set off with the usual suwarry to pay a visit to the Peshwa at his country-house, the Hira Bag. The road for a considerable distance was covered by his Highness's suwarry, chiefly horsemen, so that it was rather difficult to get to the gate ; fortunately I had a party of sepoys from the lines, who joined on the opposite bank of the river, and made way for me. It is prettily situated on the bank of a very large tank, perfectly irregular in its shape. In the centre is a small island with a pagoda. The opposite bank rises gradually into a sugar loaf hill, the summit of which is capped by the white buildings of the pagoda dedicated to

Parbuttee. The house itself is insignificant, and has never been finished. The garden is fine, and is ornamented with several noble mango trees, and a great number of cocoanut trees, which I had seen nowhere else above the Gauts, and which several people told me would not grow there. The guddy was placed in a verandah, opening to a bason of water, with fountains, and covered by a trellis of vines.

"We soon had notice to move upstairs; the Peshwa passing through a back door, while we mounted, by a narrow staircase, to a platform with two verandahs, one at each end. In the farther a white cloth was spread, on which were plantain leaves equal in number to the English gentlemen present. On each was a Brahmin's dinner, consisting of rice, plain and sweet, pastry thin as paper, and rolled up, pastrycakes, bread, and peas pudding. Along one side was a range of sweetmeats, laid in a row, having the appearance of paints on a pallet; on the other were seven different kinds of curried vegetables. On one side of the leaf were rice milk, ghee, and some other liquids, in small pans of plantain leaf, which were all excellent of their kinds. We had taken the precaution to bring spoons, knives, and forks, which we used actively out of respect to our host, who soon joined the party by seating himself on the guddy, a little on the outside of the verandah. Of course, he could not contaminate himself by eating in our presence.

"On giving notice that we had finished, he retired and we soon followed. After seating ourselves below, the betel was laid at his feet and served round."

Another distinguished personage who was received here was the gallant soldier General Wellesley afterwards the Duke of Wellington. It is recorded in the Peshwa's diary that a grand fête was given in his honour by the Peshwa Bajirao II, at Hirabag in March 1804 when the dresses of honour were presented to the General and his staff as follows :—

	Rs.	a.	p.
General Wellesley	455	0	0
Mr. Webb	376	8	0
Col. Coleman	361	8	0
Mr. Goodwin	182	0	0
Major Easden	206	12	0
Capt. Bucknell	174	14	0
Lt. Young	180	14	0
Capt. Knox	133	12	0

	Rs.	a.	p.
Capt. Campbell	134	0	0
Dr. Wales	137	8	0
Mr. Iskarell (*sic*)	137	14	0
Mr. Close	128	10	0
Mr. Bellingham	136	8	0
Govindrao	247	8	0
Apparao	179	7	0
Ramrao	49	8	0
Subbarao	36	10	0

Hirabag has up to this day maintained the reputation of being a charming place for entertainments to distinguished guests at Poona.

Besides the Government gardens there were many private gardens belonging to several notable sardars such as Nana Phadnavis, Moraba Dada, Haripant Phadke and others. Out of these Moraba Dada's garden was considered to be the best. These gardens had rendered Poona at one time a most charming and attractive city which was aptly termed "the Garden of the Deccan."

The display of fire works was the concluding part of every entertainment given by the Peshwas and the Parvati Lake was the usual place fixed for it. On such occasions the Peshwa and his guests used to go to the Parvati hill to see the fireworks. In modern times the art of fireworks or pyrotechny has been considerably improved by the progress of science and the Maratha fireworks cannot be compared with it. Luckily a list of the Maratha fireworks displayed in the times of the Peshwa has been discovered from which one can see that the Marathas were not as behind as we might suppose in that art. The old names of Maratha fireworks were as follows :—

1. *Tavdani Roshnai*—These were illuminations fixed to arches of glass with hanging mirrors.

2. *Akashmandal Tarangan*—They were just like Roman Candles filled with layers of composition and stars alternately. They were discharged like stars several feet into the air and produced a beautiful effect in various colours.

3. *Narali Jhade*—or cocoa-nut trees—These made a thundering sound like gun-fire and displayed sparks, crackers, serpents, flowers, etc., in different colours.

4. *Prabha Chamak*—Just like modern Firing Wheels giving brilliant effect of gold and silver.

Besides these there were many sorts of rockets, birds, flowers, plants, which gave beautiful effect through their various designs and colours.

Printed by E. G. Pearson at the Times Press, Bombay, and published by Rao Bahadur D. B. Parasnis, Poona.—J. 6030·21